IF ALL YO
TO LOSE

THIS IS THE BOOK FOR YOU.

GALA

FROM FAT TO FIT

(Includes a four-week exercise-course to make the body slim and shapely)

By

Dr. Dhiren Gala
B.Sc., D.H.M.S., D.O., D.Ac., C.G.O., C.C.H., A.R.S.H.

With

Dr. D. R. Gala
N.D., D.N.O., D.C.O.

Dr. Sanjay Gala
M.B. (BOM.), M.S. (ENT)

NAVNEET PUBLICATIONS (INDIA) LIMITED

G 4506

Visit us at : www.navneet.com | e-mail : npil@navneet.com

Price : R

NAVNEET PUBLICATIONS (INDIA) LIMITED

Mumbai : 1. Bhavani Shankar Road, Dadar, **Mumbai – 400 028.**
(Tel. 6662 6565 • Fax : 6662 6470)

2. **Navyug Distributors :** Road No. 8, M. I. D. C., Next to Indian Institute of Packaging, Marol, Andheri (East), **Mumbai – 400 093.**
(Tel. 2821 4186 • Fax : 2835 2758)

Ahmadabad : Navneet House, Gurukul Road, Memnagar, **Ahmadabad – 380 052.**
(Tel. 6630 5000)

Bengalooru : Sri Balaji's, No. 12, 2nd Floor, 3rd Cross, Malleswaram, **Bengalooru – 560 003.** (Tel. 2346 5740)

Chennai : 30, Sriram Nagar, North Street, Alwarpet, **Chennai – 600 018.**
(Tel. 2434 6404)

Delhi : 2-E/23, Orion Plaza, 2nd & 3rd Floor, Jhandewalan Extn., **New Delhi – 110 055.** (Tel. 2361 0170)

Hyderabad : Kalki Plaza, Plot No. 67, Krishnapuri Colony, West Maredpalley, **Secunderabad – 500 026.** (Tel. 2780 0146)

Kolkata : 1st Floor, 7, Suren Tagore Road, **Kolkata – 700 019.** (Tel. 2460 4178)

Nagpur : 63, Opp. Shivaji Science College, Congress Nagar, **Nagpur – 440 012.**
(Tel. 242 1522)

Nashik : Dharmaraj Plaza, Old Gangapur Naka, Gangapur Road, **Nashik – 422 005.** (Tel. 231 0627)

Navsari : 3/C, Arvind Nagar Society, Lunsikui Road, **Navsari – 396 445.**
(Tel. 244 186)

Patna : 1st Floor, 36-D, Sahdeo Mahto Marg, Srikrishnapuri, **Patna – 800 001.**
(Tel. 254 0321)

Pune : Navneet Bhavan, 1302, Shukrawar Peth, Near Sanas Plaza, Bajirao Road, **Pune – 411 002.** (Tel. 2443 1007)

Surat : 1, Ground Floor, Sri Vallabh Complex, Kotwal Street, Nanpara, **Surat – 395 001.** (Tel. 246 3927)

Vadodara : F-1, Vaidya Vatika, Opp. Hanuman Wadi, Sardar Bhuvan Khancho, **Vadodara – 390 001.**

[1–9–2007 (16) : 4]

PREFACE

The prevalence of obesity is rising at an alarming pace in the elite class of our society. The presence of a large number of obese persons at social functions and get-togethers is becoming a common sight.

Obesity is not just a physical condition but it is also a disease. It is a disease in the treatment of which a patient can help himself more than his physician can. For this, it is essential that the patient should know all the details about obesity.

This book contains complete information about obesity and a scientific analysis of facts supported by the statistical data.

This is a unique book in the sense that here an effort is made to make the book exhaustive on the subject by including in it almost all the important advances, made in the field of the treatment of obesity, coupled with the findings of worldwide medical research carried out in the last fifty years.

We are grateful to Dr. Babalal N. Parikh for his valuable suggestions.

We request experts on this subject and our readers to send us their reactions and valuable suggestions.

–Authors

Dr. D. R. Gala

1st floor, Abbas Building 'A',
Near Tilak Market, Jalbhai Lane, Harkishandas Hospital Road,
Grant Road (East), Mumbai–400 004.
Phone : 2386 7275 Time : 4.00 to 7.00 pm

The only book of its kind showing scientific and sure ways to make your body slim and shapely.

CONTENTS

SECTION 1 : PRIMARY INFORMATION ABOUT OBESITY

SECTION 2 : TREATMENT OF OBESITY

SECTION 3 : SOME OTHER IMPORTANT TOPICS

FROM FAT TO FIT

SECTION 1

Primary information about obesity

1. Introduction
2. Methods to detect obesity
3. Hazards of obesity
4. Gains of removing obesity
5. The causes of obesity

Proper dieting and proper exercise—a combination without which a shapely body is impossible.

1. INTRODUCTION

(Note : Terms 'Excess Fat' and 'Obesity' are employed as synonyms throughout the book.)

It is an irony of fate that on this earth on one hand millions do not get enough food and on the other, there are many more who, besides overeating, lead a sedentary life and march towards an untimely death.

In this wonderful world there have been people with wonderful weight records. Robert Hughes, an American youth, weighed 483 kg. Yes sir, nothing less than 1062 pounds! When his heart, tired of pumping blood to nooks and corners of his large body stopped beating, he was only 32. Perry Pearl, again an American, weighed 798 pounds. Her name finds a place even in the world famous 'Guinness Book of World Records'. But Mrs. Prescilla Molef outshines all of them. She weighs 1100 pounds. She has to rely upon a lorry as the only mode of transport. Vyankat Swami, a rice-eating poojari of a temple in Tamil Nadu, weighed 800 pounds. When he walked, light tremors rocked the whole area. More people came for his 'darshan' than for the darshan of the deity. At last, the deity got displeased and called him to heaven. At that time, he was only 42! Famous rock singer Elvis Presley also died due to obesity at the age of 42.

Obesity is a physical state that causes constant anxiety. It not only shortens the life-span of a person but makes his life miserable by causing many grave diseases, such as, high blood pressure, osteoarthritis and diabetes. Obesity adversely affects a person's efficiency and prevents him from participating in many activities. Sometimes, it causes psychological disorders also. Illnesses and disabilities caused by obesity outnumber all the diseases of vitamin and mineral deficiencies put together.

Obesity is an offshoot of the modern age of machines and materialism. If all the people occupying top positions in various walks of life were to assemble in one place, wearing a pair of shorts, it would present a ludicrous sight. Looking at those rotund figures with sagging bellies and masses of fat deposited at various places on their bodies, we would find it difficult to decide whether they are human beings or some funny animals!

This description is not meant to poke fun at the cost of obese persons. It is only an attempt to view the situation objectively and show how the society looks down upon them. When fat persons lose their weight through efforts and make their bodies proportional, the whole world looks at them with respect and honour.

Even if there are no apparent difficulties or handicaps in the beginning, the fat person should not presume that he is healthy or free from any dangers. The long-term dangers of obesity are like a sword hanging over one's head which can strike any time and create numerous difficulties and boundless misery.

2. METHODS TO DETECT OBESITY

The growth of a person's body is complete by the time he attains the age of 25. So, in principle, there should be no weight gain after a person reaches the age of 25. Some experts even maintain that there should be no major changn the weight of a person after he reaches the age of 20 to 22. To support their belief these experts present authentic figures and data. Dr. Slome[1] and his colleagues say that the weight of people of Zulu tribe living mainly on grain, milk and fruit, remains stable after they reach adulthood. Dr. Gastineau[2] and the Metropolitan Insurance Co. of U.S.A.[3] also endorse this view and say that after a person attains adulthood, there are no major changes in his weight.

Barring exceptional developments like pregnancy, accumulation of fluids in the body (which takes place due to some problems of endocrine glands, liver, kidneys or heart), or unnatural and malignant growth of bones, the only other factor responsible for weight gain after attaining adulthood is accumulation of fat.

The human body is made up of several different constituents which discharge different functions from the viewpoint of metabolism. They are as follows:

(1) Active cells (approx. 58 %) (2) Extra-cellular water (approx. 23 %) (3) Bones and minerals (approx. 4 %) and (4) Fat (approx. 15 %)[4]. With advancing age if physical activity decreases and the teenage eating habits continue, then fat starts accumulating and manifests itself in the form of obesity.

Obesity is that state of the body in which weight of the body is higher, at least, by 10 % than the ideal or desirable weight. If the weight is higher by 20 %, it is a state of severe obesity. It is an undisputable fact that the hazards associated with obesity are directly proportional to the amount of accumulated fat.

From the above definition the question that naturally arises is, what should be considered as the ideal or desirable weight?

Ideal weight is that which increases a person's longevity. Based on the study and survey of millions of policyholders, life insurance companies have issued charts of ideal weight. Such charts have different columns for people with different types of body-frames. Ideal weight is classified under three such columns: small frame, medium frame and large frame.

Fig. 1 : Relation of weight of the body-frame

People having the same height, but having different types of physical frames have different ideal weights. The following tables were published by the Metropolitan Insurance Co. of the United States in 1959. They are based on extensive survey and deep research and are therefore universally accepted.

IDEAL WEIGHT CHART FOR MEN AGED 25 AND ABOVE

Height		Small frame weight in		Medium frame weight in		Large frame weight in	
Cm	Ft.-inch.	Pounds	Kg	Pounds	Kg	Pounds	Kg
158	5′ 2″	111 to 120	50.5 to 54.5	118 to 129	53.5 to 58.5	126 to 141	57 to 64
160	3″	115 to 123	52 to 56	121 to 133	55 to 61	129 to 144	58.5 to 65
163	4″	118 to 126	53.5 to 57	124 to 136	56 to 62	132 to 148	60 to 67
165	5″	121 to 129	55 to 58.5	127 to 139	57.5 to 63	135 to 152	61 to 69
168	6″	124 to 133	56 to 60	130 to 143	58.5 to 65	138 to 156	62.5 to 71
170	7″	128 to 137	58 to 62	134 to 147	60 to 66.5	142 to 161	64.5 to 73
173	8″	132 to 141	60 to 64	138 to 152	62.5 to 69	147 to 166	66.5 to 75
175	9″	136 to 145	62 to 66	142 to 156	64.5 to 71	151 to 169	68.5 to 77
178	10″	140 to 150	63.5 to 68	146 to 160	66 to 72.5	155 to 174	70 to 79
180	11″	144 to 154	65 to 70	150 to 165	68 to 75	159 to 179	72 to 81
183	6′ 0″	148 to 158	67 to 71.5	154 to 170	70 to 77	164 to 184	74 to 83.5
185	1″	152 to 162	69 to 73.5	157 to 175	71.5 to 79	168 to 189	76 to 85.5
188	2″	156 to 167	71 to 76	162 to 180	73.5 to 81.5	173 to 194	78.5 to 88
190	3″	160 to 171	72.5 to 77.5	167 to 185	76 to 84	178 to 199	80.5 to 90.5
193	4″	164 to 175	74 to 79	172 to 190	78 to 86	182 to 204	82.5 to 92.5

IDEAL WEIGHT CHART FOR WOMEN AGED 25 AND ABOVE

Height		Small frame weight in		Medium frame weight in		Large frame weight in	
Cm	Ft.-inch.	Pounds	Kg	Pounds	Kg	Pounds	Kg
147	4′ 10″	92 to 98	42 to 44.5	96 to 107	43.5 to 48.5	104 to 119	47 to 54
150	11″	94 to 101	42.5 to 46	98 to 110	44.5 to 50	106 to 122	48 to 55
152	5′ 0″	96 to 104	43.5 to 47	101 to 113	46 to 51	109 to 125	49.5 to 56.5
155	1″	99 to 107	45 to 48.5	104 to 116	47 to 52.5	112 to 128	51 to 58
158	2″	102 to 110	46.5 to 50	107 to 119	48.5 to 54	115 to 131	52 to 59.5
160	3″	105 to 113	47.5 to 51	110 to 122	50 to 55	118 to 134	53.5 to 61
163	4″	108 to 116	49 to 52.5	113 to 126	51 to 57	121 to 138	55 to 62
165	5″	111 to 119	50.5 to 54	116 to 130	52.5 to 58.5	125 to 142	57 to 64.5
168	6″	114 to 123	52 to 56	120 to 135	54.5 to 61	129 to 146	58.5 to 66
170	7″	118 to 127	53.5 to 57.5	124 to 139	56 to 63	133 to 150	60 to 68
173	8″	122 to 131	55 to 59.5	128 to 143	58 to 65	137 to 154	62 to 70
175	9″	126 to 135	57 to 61	132 to 147	60 to 66.5	141 to 158	64 to 71.5
178	10″	130 to 140	58.5 to 63.5	136 to 151	62 to 68.5	145 to 163	66 to 74
180	11″	134 to 144	61 to 65	140 to 155	63.5 to 70	149 to 168	67.5 to 76
183	6′ 0″	139 to 148	63 to 67	144 to 159	65 to 72	153 to 173	69.5 to 78.5

Graphs can also be used to ascertain whether a person is underweight or overweight.

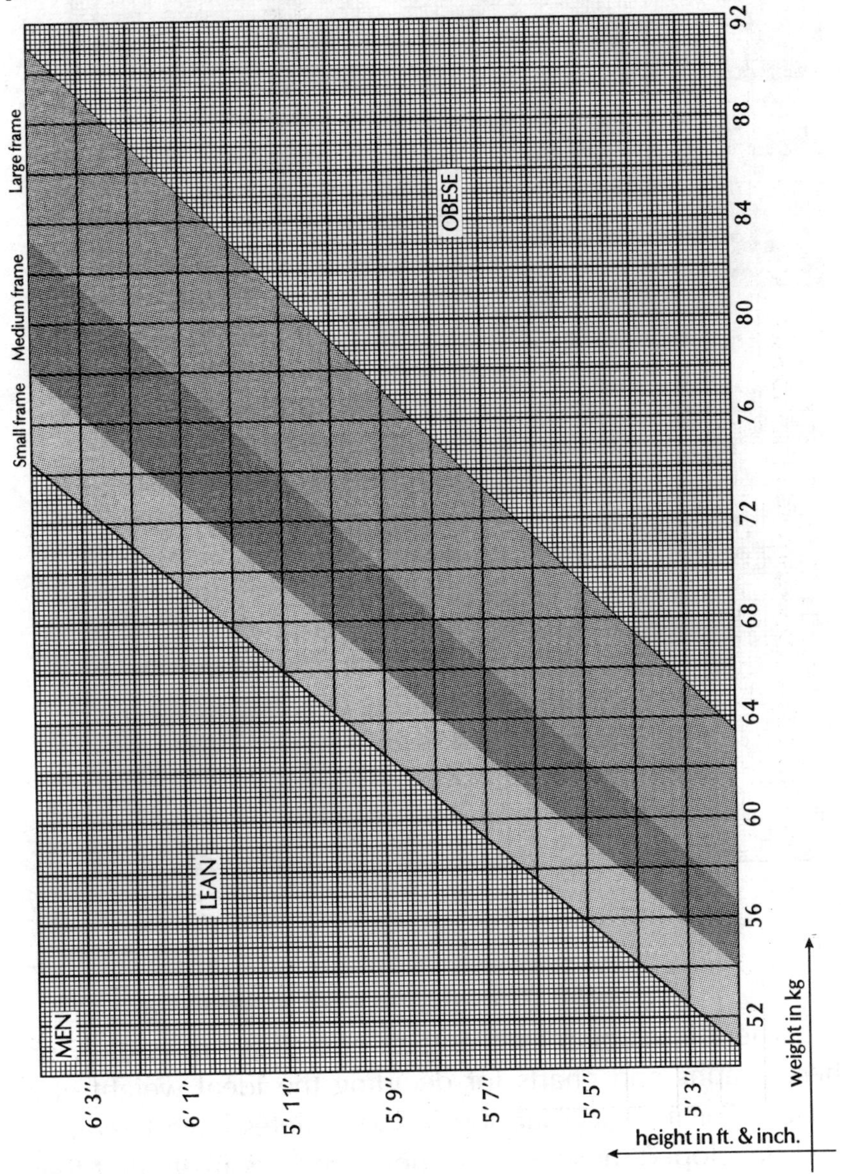

Fig. 2 : Graph showing desirable weight for men

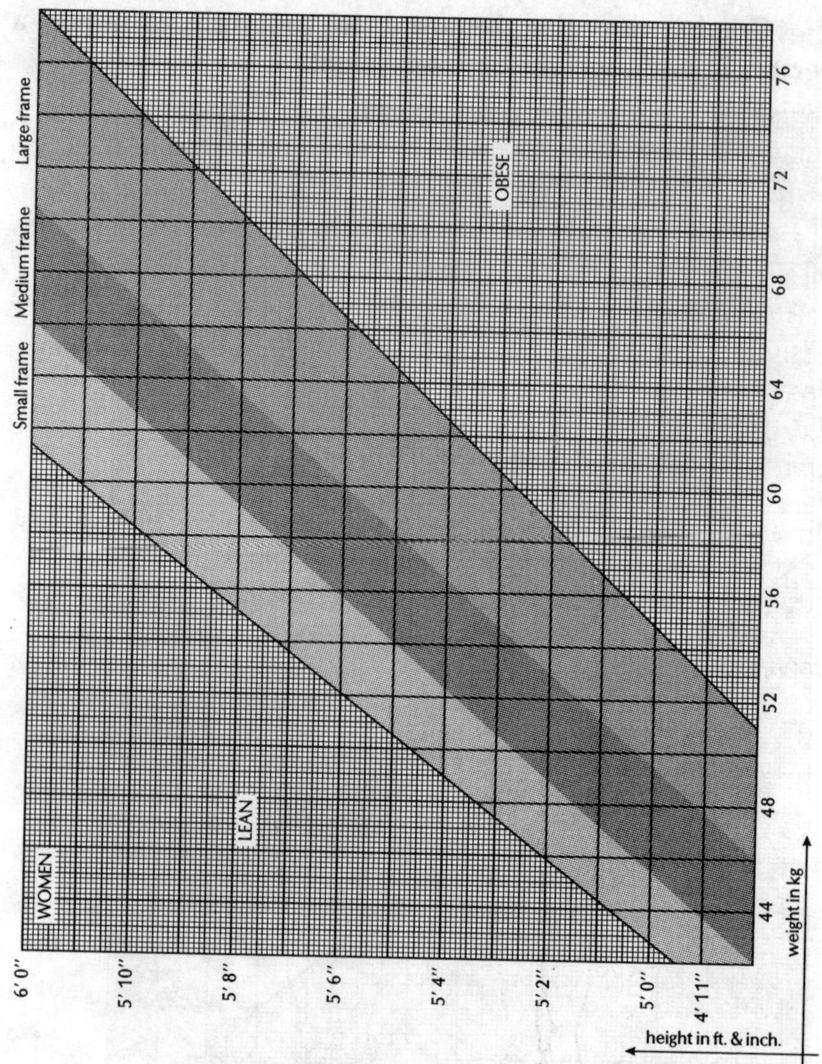

Fig. 3 : Graph showing desirable weight for women

There is scope for making an error if we rely solely on these graphs and charts for deciding the ideal weight of a person. For instance, labourers and athletes have large and well-developed muscles, and therefore, it is likely that they might weigh more for their height than the ideal weight as suggested in the table. On the other hand, muscles of those who lead a sedentary life are underdeveloped and soft.

They may be fat, though their weight might tally with the ideal weight suggested in the table. It is, therefore, not advisable to rely solely on the table to decide whether a person is obese or not. There are some other methods to do so and they should also be applied.

Other methods to ascertain the presence of excess fat :

(A) First method : Harpenden callipers are specially designed forks to pinch certain parts of the body to determine the skin-fold thickness. One of the portions of the body shown in the figure given below is pinched with that fork to ascertain the quantum of fat.

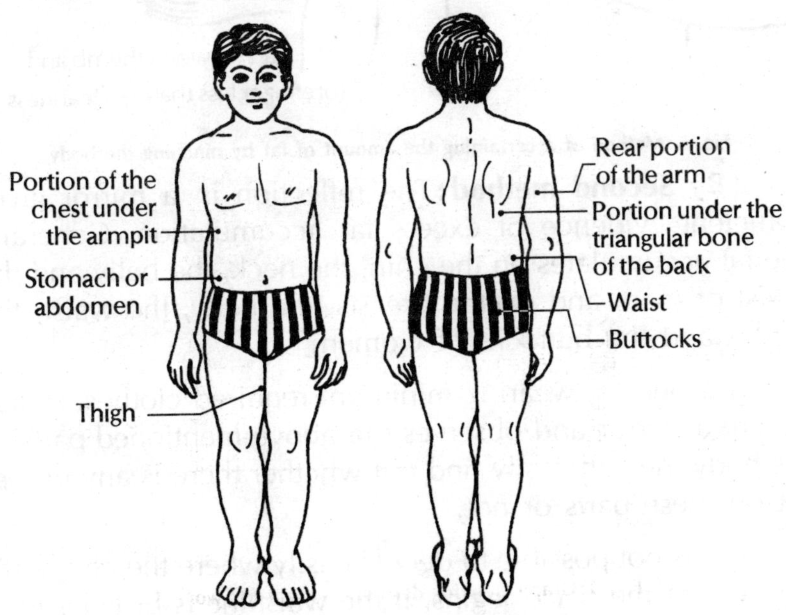

Fig. 4 : Portions of the body for pinching

After pinching the body, if the skin-fold thickness measures more than one inch, it indicates excess fat[5]. However, it is possible to ascertain excess fat even without using this specially designed instrument. Anybody can pinch his body with the help of his thumb and forefinger and can easily ascertain the presence of excess fat.

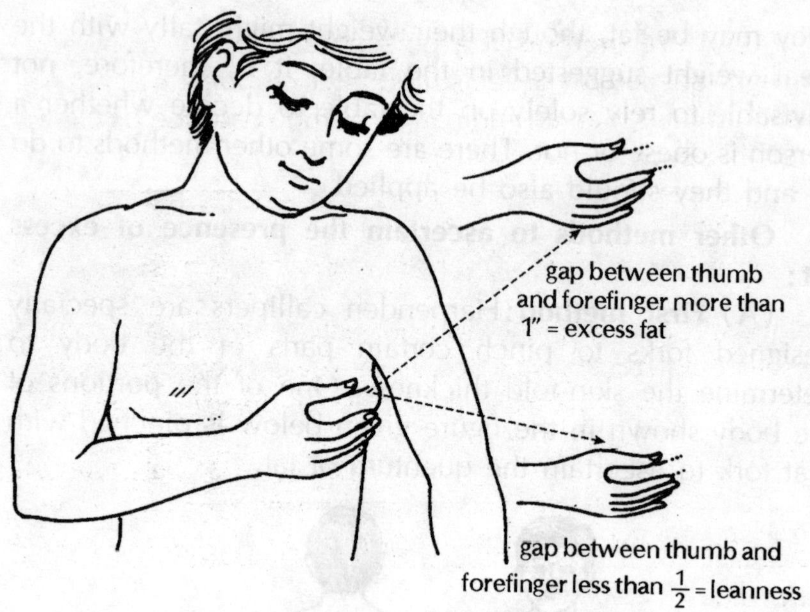

Fig. 5 : Method of ascertaining the amount of fat by pinching the body

(B) Second method : The reflection in a mirror gives sufficient evidence of excess fat accumulation. Generally the fat accumulates on the chin, the neck, the belly and the waist of men, and on the breasts, the belly, the waist, the thighs and the buttocks of women.

If a person, wearing minimum required clothes, stands before a mirror and observes the above-mentioned parts of his body, he can easily find out whether there is any excess fat on these parts or not.

If it is not possible to decide easily where the chin ends and where the neck begins, if the waistline is broader than the chestline, if the belly is large and sagging or if the thighs rub against each other while walking, they are sure signs of the excess fat. Experts believe that for men, measurement of the waistline is like a lighthouse signal. 'If one finds it difficult to put on his old clothes, or if he finds it difficult to button them up or if he feels that his clothes have started fitting him tight, it is an indication that his fat is increasing.'

(C) Third method: If a person gets breathless even at the slightest exertion or feels tired after climbing a staircase, he should take it as an indication of the presence of excess fat on his body.

Synopsis:

1. Any weight gain that occurs after the age of 20 is generally due to excess fat.
2. If your weight is 10% higher than the ideal weight, you are fat and if it is higher by 20% or more, you are obese.
3. The method of pinching the skin is very useful to ascertain obesity.
4. Standing before the mirror and observing your chin, neck, chest, belly, waist, thighs and buttocks will give you a fairly comprehensive idea of your obesity.

References:

1. Slome, C., Gampel, B., Abramson, J. H. and Scotch, N. (1960): Weight, height and skinfold thickness of Zulu adults in Durban, *S. Afr. Med. J*, 34, 505.
2. Gastineau, C.F. (1972). Obesity: Risks, causes and treatment, *Med. Clinics of N. America*, 56, 1021.
3. Metropolitan Life Insurance Co. (1943) *Statistical Bulletin, 24-6.*
4. Keys, A, (1951) *Handbook of Nutrition*, 2nd Edition, The Blackiston Co., Philadelphia.
5. Durnin, J.V. G.A. & Womersley, J. (1974). Body fat assessed from total body density and its estimation from skinfold thickness, *Br. J Nutr.* 32, 77.
6. Bjorntorp, P.(1976). in *Clin. Endocr. Metab.*, 5, 2, 431.

3. HAZARDS OF OBESITY

[People in our country are still not fully aware of the hazards associated with obesity. Detailed information about these hazards is given here with a view to focussing attention on their dreadfulness.]

No doctor has ever filled the 'cause of death' column in any death certificate with the remark 'obesity'. Diseases like heart attack, diabetes, cancer, renal disorder or haemorrhage are generally the causes of a fat person's death. Obesity, though not directly responsible for causing death, certainly causes many such dangerous diseases which in turn cause premature passing away of a person.

This nexus between obesity and various grave diseases has been conclusively established through extensive research and numerous experiments. The following details clearly indicate how obesity affects different organs and systems of the human body.

(1) Muscles: Muscles of a fat person are soft and weak. Generally even when a person is not engaged in any physical activity, some of the fibres of his muscles are in a contracted state. Such a slightly contracted state of the muscles is called the 'muscle tone'. It is due to this 'muscle tone' that we are able to translate instantly our thoughts into action. In case of obese persons, this muscle tone is very weak. Besides this, in the case of an obese person, the co-ordination between muscles and the nervous system is also inadequate. Consequently, they (fat persons) are slow in their reflex actions. As a result of this, they are more prone to injuries and accidents. It is a matter of common experience that plump babies tumble down more frequently.

A fat person consumes more energy for doing any physical work. This affects his efficiency. You can well imagine how much energy a fat person has to spend in order to carry the load of two heavy suitcases in the form of his heavy buttocks and his pot-belly weighing 10 to 12 kg! It is no wonder that a fat person gets breathless after the slightest physical exertion. Therefore fat persons are generally found to be lazy or inactive.

If the muscles are loose and weak, they cannot support the internal organs of the body and therefore they (i.e., the organs) do not remain secure in their proper positions and easily get displaced. Therefore obese persons often become victims of different types of hernia.

(2) Joints and bones: Fat persons complain of severe pain in the feet or soles which are crushed under the weight of their heavy bodies. Fat persons also suffer from flat feet. Similarly, weight-bearing joints like the ankles, hips and the spinal cord are also strained constantly on account of the heavy weight they have to carry. Consequently, fat persons are susceptible to degenerative diseases like osteoarthritis[1,2] at a very young age. Therefore persons who complain of constant pain in the knees are advised to reduce weight.

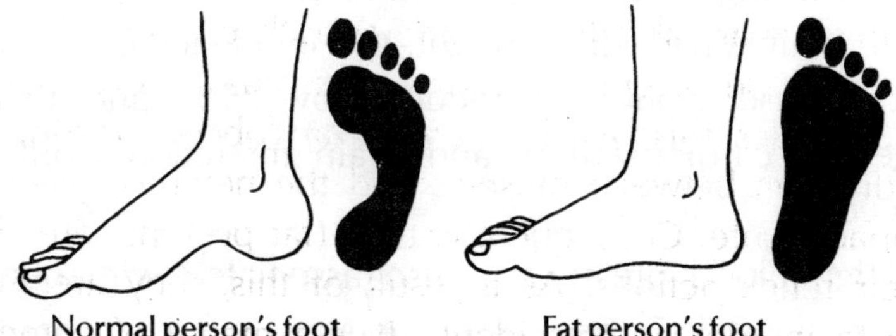

Fig. 6: Effect of obesity on the feet

All the joints of the body are surrounded by muscles. Muscles lend support to the joints. As the muscles of a fat person are weak, their joints are not adequately supported. This is the main reason why fat persons often complain of chronic backache.

Besides this, the joints of a fat person are stiff and therefore, their bodies are less flexible and they cannot bend their bodies easily.

Compared to normal children, fat children are more prone to congenital and acquired deformities of bones and joints. According to Dr. Hodgekin[3], compared to normal people, fat persons are more prone to fractures, dislocations and other grave injuries to arms and legs.

(3) The cardiovascular system : Generally the level of cholesterol is high in the blood of fat people. With the passage of time, this cholesterol gets deposited on the inner surface of blood vessels. As a result of this, blood vessels not only become hard and narrow, but also lose their elasticity. Dr. Wilens[4] who has performed thousands of post-mortems says that 75 % of the victims of hardened blood vessels are fat. Like other blood vessels, arteries which supply blood to the heart, are also narrowed in the case of fat people. Such a situation creates circumstances conducive to ischemic heart disease.

According to Dr. Gordon and Dr. Kennel, if all the people maintained ideal weight, the incidence of coronary heart disease would be reduced by 25 % and that of congestive cardiac failure and brain infarction would be reduced by 35 %.

High blood pressure is also associated with obesity. After studying 567 cases of fat persons and 1225 cases of normal persons, Dr. Pincherle and Dr. Wright[5] have stated that the number of fat persons suffering from high blood pressure is $2\frac{1}{2}$ times more than that of normal persons.

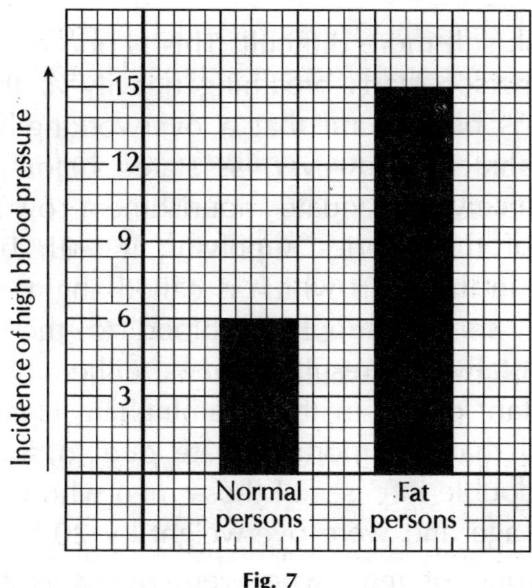

Fig. 7

Based on their study of the physical examination of 74,000 industrial workers, Dr. Dublin and Dr. Marks[6] maintain that heavier the person, higher is his blood pressure. In the case of a fat person, high blood pressure develops at an early age. Sometimes, it develops as early as the second decade of the life-span. This is a very grave fact. After studying numerous cases of 12 to 15 year-old students of schools in New York, Dr. Christakis[7] says that among the fat children, blood pressure of 19.7% children was higher than the desired level.

Fat persons are more prone to thrombophlebitis and varicose veins.[8] Varicose veins are an indication of slow blood circulation.

Nature has given human beings a heart which is fit to serve the body of a normal size only. It is not meant to serve very heavy bodies. In fact, a fat person can be compared to a monster bearing the heart of a midget. The heart has to work very hard to supply blood to every nook and corner of a heavy body. Thickened veins and arteries make its task still more difficult. This is one of the reasons why a fat person starts breathing heavily at the slightest exertion. It is but natural that a overworking-heart needs more nourishment. However, as stated before, the heart does not receive adequate nourishment owing to the narrowing of the arteries supplying it with blood. This causes pain in the heart which is called angina pectoris. If one of the arteries supplying blood to the heart gets obstructed totally, the result could be either a heart attack or even instant death. In the 'Framingham Heart Study' it was noticed that the mortality rate due to sudden heart attack was double in cases of those men who were around 40 years of age and were overweight by 20 %.

In a group of men who were overweight by 25 %, 15 % men had abnormal electrocardiograms.[10] Many fat persons die premature deaths due to degenerative heart diseases.[11]

(4) The respiratory system : The act of breathing involves the movement of several parts of the chest and stomach. Two types of muscles are mainly responsible for this : (1) some muscles of the chest and (2) the diaphragm. When a fat person breathes, he has to lift his heavy chest every time, and besides this, he also finds it difficult to push the diaphragm towards the fat-stuffed belly and stomach. It is because of this that a fat person gets tired and breathless easily.

Tight apparels worn to hide the fat are also responsible for heavy breathing to certain extent. A tight vest does not allow the chest to expand fully and a pair of tight-fitting trousers at the waist prevents the diaphragm from coming down.

Thus, the breathing of a fat person is shallow. Because of this, on one hand he does not get adequate quantity of oxygen and on the other hand carbon dioxide from his body is not fully expelled. So, his body becomes a storehouse of poisons.

(5) The digestive system : It has been noticed that the proportion of cholesterol is high in the blood of fat persons. This high cholesterol causes stone formation in the gall-bladder. Some other disorders of the gall-bladder also bother fat persons.[12] Out of the men dying due to disorders of the gall-bladder, 75 % are overweight.[13, 14]

The liver too is adversely affected by obesity. It has been found that degenerative diseases of the liver and cirrhosis of liver strike obese[15] persons more often.

More fat persons are found to be suffering from intestinal diseases like diverticular disease of colon[16] and other ailments like piles. Based on their study of 7,50,000 fat persons, Dr. Lew and Dr. Garfinkel have proved that fat persons suffer more from disorders of the digestive system than those who are normal.[17]

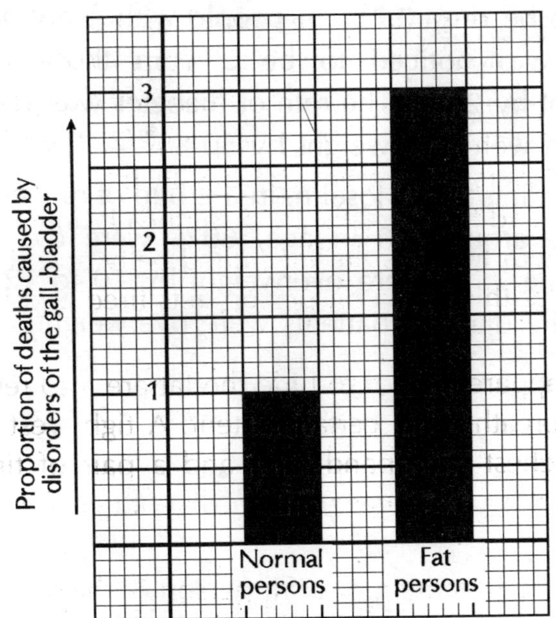

Fig. 8

(6) The reproductive system : The married life of obese persons is often a tragic tale. The extra fat in their body adversely affects their nerves and endocrine glands. Fat women suffer from menorrhagia, infertility and several other disorders of menstruation.

Obesity creates many problems during pregnancy also. After conducting a survey of 641 pregnant women, Dr. O'dell and Dr. Mangert found that obesity creates many problems like toxaemia, difficulties in delivery, post-delivery bleeding, death of either the mother or the child, etc. on a large scale. Fat women, generally, do not have normal deliveries. A caesarian operation is required in the cases of most of the fat women.[18]

(7) The endocrine glands : Obesity disrupts the proper functioning of endocrine glands. The nexus between obesity and diabetes is well known. The rate of diabetes was noticed to be only 0.7 % in people with a normal weight; while it was noticed to be 2 % in those who were overweight by 20 %. The rate of diabetes was 10 % among those who were overweight by 50 %.[19]

According to Dr. Joselin, in a group of diabetic patients who were around 40 in age, 60 % were overweight by 20 %; while 25 % were overweight by 10 to 12 %. In all, 85 % of the diabetic patients were overweight.

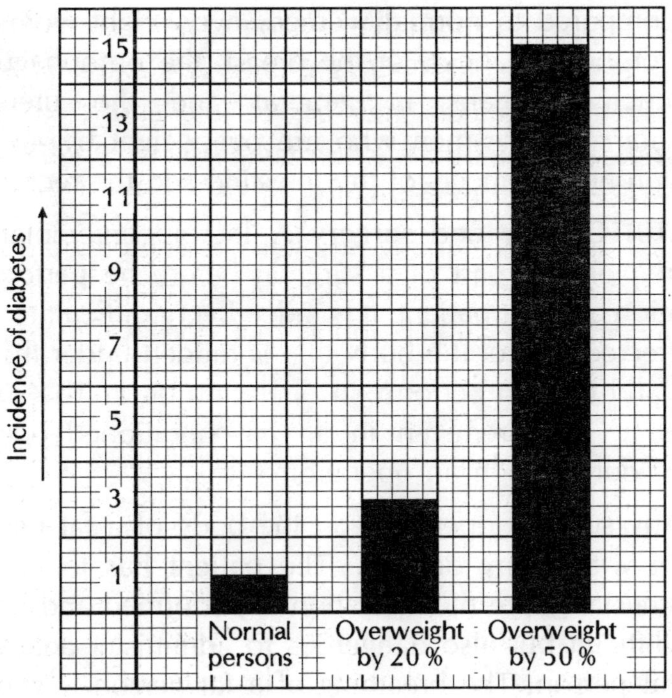

Fig. 9

(8) The excretory system: Degenerative changes in the kidneys occur more severely and early in obese persons.[20]

Fat people perspire profusely. There are two reasons for this: (1) A fat person has to spend a lot of energy to do any physical work, (2) Layers of fat deposited on the body act as woollen jackets or sweaters and cause profuse perspiration which emits a foul odour. Such foul-smelling sweat causes great embarrassment to fat people.

(9) Obesity and cancer: Possibilities of developing cancer are directly proportional to overweight. This fact applies particularly to those who are aged above 45. The rate of cancer was noticed to be higher by 10% among those who were obese.

Compared to normal women, overweight women are more prone to cancers of the breast, the oesophagus and reproductive organs in general and the uterus in particular.[21] Those men who are overweight by 40% are more prone to cancers of the intestine and the rectum.[22, 23]

(10) Obesity and surgery: A lot of contemplation is required on the part of a surgeon before he performs an operation on a fat patient. It is indeed very difficult to locate the affected part of the body that is hidden under the mass of fat and then to perform an operation on it. The surgeon begins to perspire even in an air-conditioned operation theatre during such an operation.

Any surgical operation on the body of a fat person is fraught with many dangers. The patient has to be given anaesthesia before the operation is performed and it is not only difficult but also dangerous to administer anaesthesia to a fat person. The breathing of a fat person is generally shallow as the movement of his diaphragm is hindered. Anaesthesia is likely to affect his breathing adversely. The chances of developing embolism in the veins are also more in obese.[24]

Moreover, post-surgical recovery is also very slow in fat persons. Their convalescence period is usually very long.

A surgical operation is generally effective in the treatment of diseases like gall-stones, appenditits, piles, hernia, cancer of the intestines, varicose veins, etc. But it is difficult to perform a surgical operation on fat persons. Consequently, they are deprived of the proper treatment and may die for the want of surgical treatment.

(11) Social and psychological problems: Fat persons are often made targets of fun, gossip and ridicule among friends and in the society. As a result of this, many fat persons develop an inferiority complex or suffer from other psychological disorders. They lack self-confidence and find it difficult to get along with other people because of their shyness.

Obesity also creates problems in finding a suitable life-partner, in getting a suitable job or in getting the desired types of readymade garments.

(12) Obesity and life-expectancy: Extensive research indicates that obesity is a major factor that reduces life-expectancy. Diseases caused by obesity lead a person to the gates of heaven prematurely.

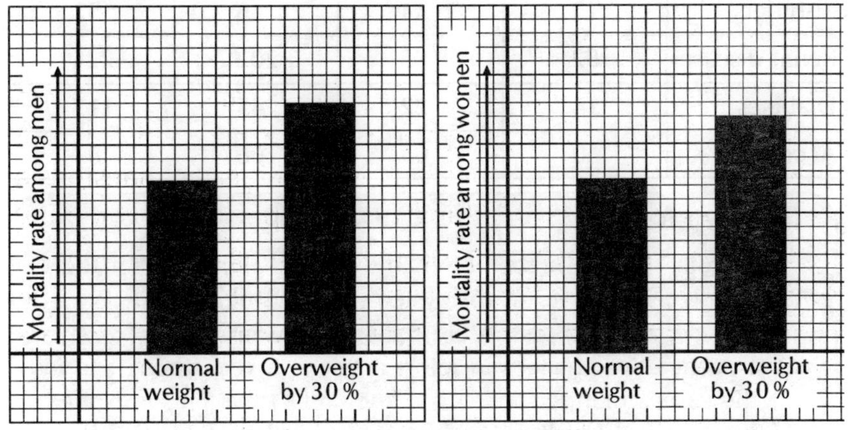

Fig. 10

'New York Metropolitan Life Insurance Co.' of the United States carried out an intensive survey of 50,000 fat persons who were required to pay higher premium due to their being overweight and has published figures of their mortality rate. An idea of relationship between high mortality rate and obesity can be obtained from an examination of these figures. In a group of persons, ranging from 40 to 70 in age, among those who were overweight by 30%, the rate of mortality was higher by 42% in the case of men and 36% in the case of women. This is an alarming fact. Given below is a table showing figures of fat people who die a premature death due to fatal diseases caused by obesity. These figures are a shocking indication of the hazards associated with obesity:

Disease	Normal weight	Overweight by 5 to 15%	Overweight by 15 to 25%	Overweight by more than 25%
	Mortality rate per 1,00,000 persons	Mortality rate per 1,00,000 persons	Mortality rate per 1,00,000 persons	Mortality rate per 1,00,000 persons
Heart attack	80	115	133	139
High B. P. and other circulatory disorders	23	34	46	51
Renal diseases	82	108	202	224
Diabetes	14	22	45	117
Accidents	60	65	66	87

Synopsis:

1. Obesity is the mother of many serious ailments. It causes major disorders in all the systems of the human body.
2. Muscles of a fat person are flabby and weak.
3. Degenerative changes in joints occur at a very young age in the cases of fat persons. It is a known fact that persons suffering from osteo-arthritis are advised to reduce their weight.
4. Blood vessels of fat persons become narrow and hard causing diseases like high blood pressure, angina pectoris and heart attacks.
5. Fat persons are more susceptible to disorders of the digestive system.
6. The married life of fat persons is pitiable.
7. A fat woman who is pregnant creates a danger not only for herself but also for the foetus.
8. The nexus between obesity and diabetes has been established conclusively.
9. Fat persons are more prone to cancer.
10. The most important fact is that obesity shortens the life span and leads to premature death.

References :

1. Cecil, R. L. (1943)–A *Textbook of Medicine by American authors,* 6th Edition, W. B. Saunders Co.; Philadelphia.
2. Faust, R. A. (1946)–Complications of Obesity, *New Orleans M. & S. J.,* 98 : 502.
3. Hodgekin, K. (1973)–*Towards earlier diagnosis,* 3rd edition, Churchill Livingston, Edinburgh.
4. Wilens, S. L. (1947)–Bearing of General Nutritional State on Atherosclerosis, *Arch. Int. Med.,* 79 : 129.
5. Pincherle, G. & Wright, H. Beric (1967)–Screening in the early diagnosis and prevention of cardiovascular disease. *J. Coll. gen. Practit.,* 13, 280.
6. Master, A. M., Dublin, L. I. & Marks, H. H. (1950)–The normal blood-pressure range and its clinical implications, *J. A. M. A.* 143 : 1464.
7. Christakis, G., Miriajanian, A., Narth, L., Khurana, H.S., Cowell, C., Archer, M., Frank, 0., Ziffer, H., Baker, H. & James, G. (1968)–A nutritional epidemiologic investigation of 642 New York City children. *Am. J. Clin. Nutr.,* 21, 107.
8. Burkitt, D. P. (1972)–Varicose veins, deep vein thrombosis and haemorrhoids : epidemiology and suggested aetiology, *Br. Med. J. ii, 556.*
9. Gordon, T. & Kannel, W. B. (1973)–The effect of overnight on cardiovascular disease. Geriatrics, 28, 80.
10. Short, J. J. (1939)–The increase in electro-cardiographic changes with obesity, *Proc. Life Ext. Examiners,* 1 : 82.
11. Dublin, L. I. (1930)-The influence of weight on certain causes of death, *Human Biol.,* 2 : 159.
12. Dublin, L. I., Jimmis, A. 0. & Marks. H. H. (1934)–Factors in the selection of risks with a history of gall-bladder disease, *Proc. Assoc. Life Ins. Med. Dir. America,* 21 : 34.
13. Marks, H. H. (1960)–Influence of Obesity in Morbidity and Mortality, *Bull. N. Y. Acad. Sc.,* 36 : 296-312.
14. Friedman, G. D., Kannel, W. B. & Danber, T. R. (1966)–The epidemiology of gall-bladder disease : Observation in the Framingham Study, *J. Chron. Dis.,* 19 : 273-292.
15. Denis Craddock (1978)–*Obesity and its management,* 3rd edition, Churchill Livingston, New York.
16. Painter, N. S. (1969)–Diverticular disease of the colon–a disease of the century. *Lancet,* ii, 586.

17. Lew, E. A. & Garfinkel, L. (1979)–Variations in mortality by weight among 750,000 men and women, *J. Chron. Dis.,* 32:563-576.
18. Mathews, H. B. and Derbrucke, M. G. (1938)–Normal expectancy in the extremely obese pregnant women, *J. A. M. A.* 110:554.
19. Butterfield, W. J. H. (1973)–In *Nutritional problems in a changing world,* ed. Hollingworth, D. & Rusell, M., Applied Science Publishers, London.
20. Dublin, L. I. (1930)–The influence of weight on certain causes of death, *Human Biol.,* 2:159.
21. Hertig, A. T. & Sommers, S. C. (1949)–Genesis of endometrial carcinoma, summary of prior biopsies *Cancer.* 2:946.
22. Burkitt, D. P. (1971)–Epidemiology of cancer of the colon & the rectum, *Cancer;* 28, 3.
23. Lew, E. A. & Garfinkel, L. (1979)–Variations in mortality by weight, *J. Chron. Dis.,* 32:563-576.
24. Barker, N. W., Nygaard, K. K., Walters, W. and Priestley, J. T. (1941)–A statistical Study of post-operative venous thrombosis and pulmonary embolism. II. Predisposing factors, *Proc. Staff Meet., Mayo Clin.,* 16:1.

4. GAINS OF REMOVING OBESITY

Losing excess fat yields many gains. These gains can be divided into two categories: (1) Psychological and social gains, (2) Physical gains.

(1) Psychological and social gains: The apparent gain of the weight-loss is that there is a dramatic improvement in a person's appearance. This yields a rich psychological gain. The inferiority complex caused by obesity starts disappearing. Shyness and tendency to avoid people also begin to vanish and their place is taken by confidence and self-respect. Proportionate to the weight-loss is the gain in morale. In case of some persons, their outlook and approach to life change completely.

Generally fat persons do not enjoy proper social acceptability. They are often made targets of fun and ridicule. Once the obesity vanishes, they start acquiring a respectable position in the society. In matrimonial matters, a fat girl has little prospects; but with her obesity gone, her prospects improve dramatically.

(2) Physical gains: Yet another important gain made by losing weight is that a person's life-expectancy rises to its normal level. This fact is supported by several studies and research conducted by experts from time to time.[1] Even insurance companies recognize this fact. They accept certain applications which were rejected earlier on the ground that the person to be insured happened to be overweight.

Shedding excess fat restores a person's lost health and beauty that had been robbed away. The body becomes light and bubbling with spirit, cheerfulness and enthusiasm.

Some researches indicate that as a sequel to the reduction in obesity, high molecular lipoprotein level in the blood also drops.[2] Most experts hold a firm belief that these lipoproteins get deposited in the blood-vessels and make them hard and narrow. High blood pressure develops as a result of this process of hardening of blood-vessels. With reduction in weight, the blood pressure also drops. And therefore, it is imperative for obese patients suffering from high blood pressure to reduce their weight. With shedding of excess fat, heart begins to function smoothly and efficiently. Chances of heart attack or coronary thrombosis also decrease.

As a result of the weight-loss, the body's capacity to metabolise sugar also increases and as a result of that, chances of diabetes also decrease. If the diabetes is in its early stages, weight-loss alone is an adequate remedy and treatment with drugs like insulin can be avoided. It is the opinion of world famous physician Dr. Newburgh that sometimes the presence of sugar in the urine of a fat middle-aged person is not a symptom of diabetes, but is an indication of the accumulation of fat in the liver causing disruption in the process of glycogen production.[3]

As a result of weight-loss, complaints like dysmenorrhea, amenorrhea and other irregularities of menstruation cycle also disappear. Dr. Mitchell's experience in this regard makes an interesting study. Out of 32 fat women who had developed menopause, 15 women reduced their weight and out of them 13 started menstruating once again. While out of the remaining 17 women who did not care to reduce their weight, only 2 of them started menstruating again.[4] Infertility of many a woman has been removed as a result of weight-loss and they have been able to conceive. However, it must be borne in mind that besides obesity, there are many other factors responsible for infertility. So, weight-loss may not remove infertility in all cases. But reduction in fat yields more satisfaction in married life. It also removes men's complaint of impotency and women's complaint of frigidity.

As a result of weight-loss, a lot of burden is taken off the joints of the body in general and those of the feet in particular. There is considerable relief in the complaint of pain in the joints. It also removes stiffness of the joints and restores their movements. This facilitates a person's participation in sports and other social activities. Weight-loss also reduces the chances of osteo-arthritis. Fat women suffering from degenerative diseases of knee joints are always advised to reduce their weight.

Obesity causes certain undesirable changes in body's metabolism. They can be avoided by shedding excess fat.[5] This also reduces the chances of developing hernias in the body.

Shedding of excess fat reduces perspiration also. This is a very important social gain for a fat person. His complexion improves and his skin becomes resistant to diseases.

Some disgruntled elements sometimes try to discourage a fat person, who is trying to reduce, by painting a false picture of the consequences of his reduction programme. Their arguments are generally based on the following points:

(1) Dietary control can sometimes prove fatal.

(2) Following the reduction in weight, lustre on a person's face vanishes and it appears pale and dull.

(3) Following the reduction in fat, the skin becomes loose and flabby.

(4) Due to dieting, stomach shrinks in size and the digestive system becomes weak for ever.

(5) During the weight-loss regimen a person tends to become short-tempered and falls a victim to many other complaints such as mental weakness, fatigue, uneasiness, insomnia, etc.

A scientific refutation of these arguments is very important and hence the following points :

(1) Dieting undertaken for shedding extra fat is a matter of sensible planning. It is not senseless starvation. Care is taken to ensure that the body gets all the necessary nutrients required for maintaining health. Dieting is never a cause of death. There are many incidents on record where under experts' guidance people have successfully fasted, subsisting only on water for 2 to 3 months. If this is true, how is it that a person who eats a balanced diet would die ? Yes, a person may die due to diseases like diabetes, heart attack, cancer, etc. which are associated with obesity. But dieting cannot be blamed for death.

Obesity is the result of overeating and imbalanced diet. Dieting is a constructive step in the direction of rectifying these flaws.

(2) There is only partial truth in the statement that lustre vanishes from a person's face following the reduction in fat. In some cases, it does happen like that, but this type of paleness is only temporary and the facial complexion regains its lustre and glow very soon. Application of cream and oil massage expedite this recovery. So it is not necessary to labour under an illusion or anxiety that paleness on face will continue for a long time.

(3) Similarly, there is only partial truth in the statement that after shedding the excess fat, the skin becomes flabby and begins to sag. Even if it occurs in a few cases, it is only a temporary development. Flexibility is one of the most important qualities of the skin. The fact that skin does not acquire flabbiness even after pregnancy, dropsy or after the disappearance of oedema (swelling) proves this point.

(4) It is a ridiculous argument to say that as a result of dieting the stomach shrinks in size. Stomach is made of highly elastic tissues. The false notion that if the diet intake is reduced, the stomach is contracted, is nothing but a grave self-deception.

Dieting never makes the digestive system weak. On the contrary, it makes it more healthy and improves its efficiency. It is overeating and not dieting which is responsible for digestive disorders.

(5) There is hardly any substance in the argument that dieting makes a person ill-tempered. To say that a person who is trying to reduce his weight feels tired or depressed is nothing but a misrepresentation of fact. In reality, it is the fat person who is always a target of fun and derision. When his excess fat disappears and he looks smart and shapely, he becomes cheerful and enthusiastic. It is said that fat persons are always easy going, carefree type of people with a good sense of humour. But in reality, they have little option except to do so. A fat person who always appears happy and smiling even when he is made a target of cruel jokes and intolerable fun is actually torn by a grave internal conflict. So, it is likely that in the initial stages of his weight reduction programme, his inner conflict comes out on the surface. But with gradual reduction in fat, the very cause of fun and derision begins to disappear. People then start looking at the person with respect when they learn that he has achieved the weight-loss through serious and hard attempts. And when the very cause of internal conflict vanishes, there is no reason why a person should become ill-tempered.

It is likely that in the initial stages of dieting, unsatisfied appetite weighs heavily on a person's mind, which in turn makes him restless. But this problem subsides when the unnatural appetite itself vanishes gradually.

It is our common experience that after a heavy meal we feel lazy and sleepy. So, in the initial phase of the dieting if a person feels more energetic and less sleepy, there is no cause for concern.

In short, there is no harm if a person tries to reduce his weight scientifically and rationally. He only stands to gain many things.

Synopsis:

1. Unimaginable gains are achieved by reducing excess fat.
2. Removal of obesity elevates a person's social position.
3. Chances of developing grave diseases like high blood pressure, heart attack, diabetes, etc. are reduced.
4. Defunct menstruation cycle is reactivated following reduction in weight and prospects of conception for a sterile woman brighten up.
5. Removal of obesity enhances a person's life expectancy.
6. Planned dieting is 100% safe and has no side-effects.
7. Weight-loss does not cause flabbiness of skin; nor does it reduce lustre and glow on a person's face.
8. Shedding of excess fat generates self-confidence and helps a person in acquiring mental peace.

References:

1. Marks, H. H. (1960)–Influence of obesity on morbidity and mortality. *Bull N. Y. Acad. Med.,* 36, 296.
2. Walker, W. J. et al (1953)–Effect of weight reduction and caloric balance on serum lipoproteins and cholesterol level *Am. J. Med.,* 14.654.
3. Newborgh, L. H. & Conn, J. W. (1939)–A new interpretation of hyperglycemia in obese middle-aged persons, *J. A. M. A.,* 112.7.
4. Mitchell, G. W. & Rogers, J. (1955)–The influence of weight reduction on amenorrhoea in obese women, *New Eng. J. Med.,* 249,835.
5. Sims, E. A. H. et al (1973)–Endocrine and metabolic effects of experimental obesity in man, *Recent Prog. Horm. Res.,* 29, 451.

5. THE CAUSES OF OBESITY

(It is an undisputable fact that it is not possible to treat any illness rationally unless its cause is fully known. Research and numerous studies have been carried out with a view to fathom the aetiology of obesity. As it is an important subject, we have discussed it here in detail.)

Obesity is mainly a problem of the affluent society. It is the result of excess consumption of sweet and processed foods accompanied by the lack of adequate physical activity.

It is still a matter of unsolved mystery how is it that some people are able to maintain their weight in spite of the fact that they consume a lot of food, and how is it that some others eat only a little and yet get fat. However, compared to the data available a few years ago, a lot of further information is available today.

Before we commence our discussion on the aetiology of obesity, let us examine some useful elementary information about hunger and satiety. There are two terms which are closely associated with food. They are 'hunger' and 'appetite'. These are different concepts. There is a difference in their meaning. Hunger is generated by the body-mechanism or by the digestive system. It manifests itself through two symptoms : (1) by hunger contractions of the stomach or (2) by saliva secretion in the mouth. On the other hand, appetite is a psychological concept. It depends on a person's knowledge about food and its smell, colour, etc. Sometimes, a person tends to eat even if he is not hungry. For instance, some people can eat ice cream, paubhaji or bhelpuri soon after taking their regular meal. On the other hand, sometimes a person's hunger dies if the food offered to him is not palatable to him.

Though hunger and appetite are two different concepts, both of them invariably induce a person to eat more and as a result of that a person acquires obesity.

There are certain centres in the brain which control hunger and appetite. Some experts believe that there is a separate centre in the brain which signals satiety. These centres are located in that part of the brain which is known as thalamus.

There is no unanimity among experts regarding the process that regulates the quantity of food intake of a person. According to some, a person experiences satisfaction only when the stomach gets distended by a certain amount. Sugar is the least satisfying food item; while fatty substances bring the satisfaction soon and thereafter the appetite does not develop for a long time as the fatty substances remain in the stomach for a long time.[2]

According to another school of thought, hunger develops when the level of blood sugar goes down.[3] According to Dr. Brobeck, we eat food in order to maintain our body-temperature. When the body-temperature goes down, the hunger develops. When the food is consumed, the body temperature rises once again and feeling of satiety occurs.[4] In short, the food generates heat. This heat is known as 'Specific Dynamic Action' (S.D.A.). This S.D.A. is found to be maximum in protein food and minimum in the fatty substances. Dr. Strang and Dr. McCluggage say that S.D.A. is generated in different measures in fat persons and in normal persons. Fat persons consume more food because S.D.A. is not generated quickly in their body.[5]

In short, the process that regulates the food intake is complex and confusing. Besides the factors associated with metabolism, other factors such as food habits, environment, taste and flavour of the food items, social pressure, mental tension, etc. also affect a person's food intake.

After having gone through this preliminary discussion on the regulation of the quantity of food intake, let us proceed to discuss the possible causes of obesity. Logically speaking, there can be only one cause responsible for accumulation of excess fat in the body – and that is – overeating. The mechanism of human body is such that the food that is in excess to the quantity required for generating energy gets converted into fat and then gets deposited in the body. It is a law of Nature that if the quantity of the food intake is in proportion to the energy expended, there is no fat accumulation.

An average healthy person generally takes food just enough to meet the requirements of his energy expenditure. As a result of this, his weight remains stable. But, for some reason, if this balance is lost, the weight no longer remains stable. It is a universally recognized fact that it is this imbalance between the food intake and the energy expenditure which is responsible for causing obesity. So now the question is – which are the factors responsible for creating such an imbalance? How and why do the different systems and processes responsible for maintaining weight in normal persons fail in their function in case of obese persons?

(1) The role of genetic factors in obesity: The moot question is : Do the genetic factors play a role in causing obesity? Different experts have presented contradictory opinions on this issue. However, most of the experts hold the view that the genetic factors do play, to some extent, a role in developing obesity. It is an undeniable fact that generally the parents or the children of fat persons are also fat. After studying cases of 75 fat women, Dr. Gurney noticed that either both or one of the parents of 82% women were obese. With the help of yet another study, he has shown that (1) If both the parents are fat 73% of their children are also fat; (2) If one of the parents is fat 45 % of their children are fat; (3) If both the parents are of normal weight only 9% children appear to be fat.[6]

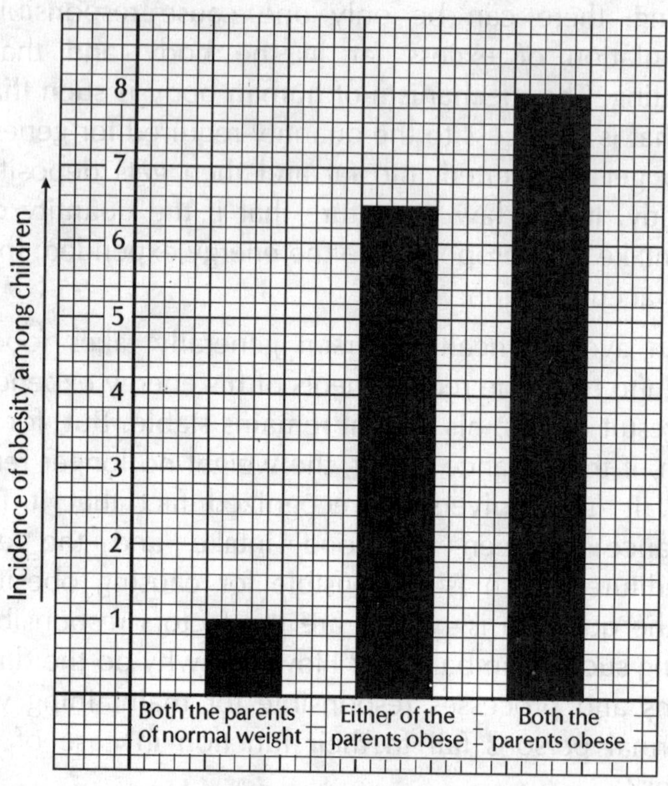

Fig. 11

It is an undeniable fact that every individual inherits his physical constitution. It is a natural phenomenon that some people have a narrow frame while some others have a broad frame. The structure of the body is closely associated with the obesity.

Some experts believe that a person inherits only the structure, that is to say, the role of genetic factor is limited only to the structure of the body and it does not extend to the obesity. Thereafter obesity develops depending upon factors like eating habits, way of life and environment.

Children generally take their meals with their parents and therefore they quickly imbibe their parents' habits. Children imitate the improper habits of their elders or fat parents, and in turn, they also become fat.

Some experts disagree with this view and present the following arguments to prove the fact that it is not only the structure that a person inherits but it is also obesity that he inherits:

(1) There has been an extensive study of identical twins. Dr. Newman and others studied 19 pairs of twins who were separated after their birth and were brought up in different environments.[8] Their study revealed that though the environment and the circumstances of those children were different, their weights were almost equal. Dr. Sheilds has also carried out a similar study.[9]

(2) It is possible that the weights of children brought up in the same environment could be different.

(3) No uniformity is noticed in the weights of real brothers and sisters, and step-brothers and sisters. Dr. Withers has shown that many a time the weights of real brothers and sisters are equal but same is not the case with step brothers and sisters.[10]

(4) Dr. Roney's study of 18 pairs of obese mothers and daughters revealed that the accumulation of fat in the body of the daughters generally occurred in the same spots where it existed in case of their mothers.

Dr. Robinson and Dr. Brucer noticed that among people with narrow frame only 3% men and 5% women were fat; while among people with broad frame 37% men and 67% women were fat.

Noted American anthropologist, Dr. Shelden says that even with the advancing age, there is not much change in the weight of people with narrow frame; but those with the broad frame keep on getting fat gradually.

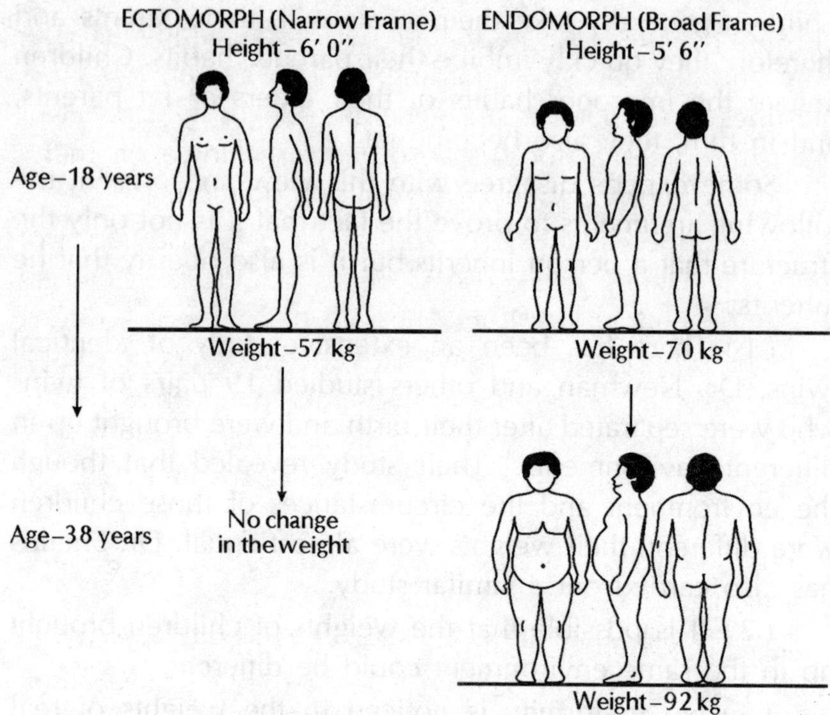

Fig. 12 : Relation of obesity to body-frame

The above-mentioned arguments make it difficult to rule out the role of genetic factors in causing obesity. So, the question that arises is : How do these factors work ? The following points are noteworthy in this regard :

Physical exertion : Fat persons are generally slow in their movements. They spend less energy in acts of sitting, getting up or walking about. Even experts have supported this view.

Food habits & the digestive system : Dr. Mall[11] says that slim and single-bodied children like only a few food items. They are fussy in their likes and dislikes about the particular food items; while fat children have liking for almost all the food items. Fat children keep on eating something or the other between meals also. Dr. Marston[12] has also made a comparative study of the food habits of fat and slim persons. He says that fat persons generally take big bites and eat faster. According to Dr. Woolley[13] small intestines of fat persons are generally longer as a result of which the digested food is absorbed fast. However, many physicians disagree with Dr. Woolley's opinion.

Endocrine glands: In some cases, disorders of endocrine glands have also been found to have caused obesity. In conclusion, it can be said that there is a strong evidence supporting the view that genetic factors do play a role in causing obesity. But at the same time, it is important to note that even genetic obesity yields to dieting and other attempts to reduce weight.[14] Further advancement of genetic obesity can be checked. Genetic obesity can even be cured. There is no reason to despair and give up the fight against obesity even if it is inherited.

(2) Psychological and social factors in obesity: In modern society, some people eat not only to satisfy their hunger, but sometimes to enjoy and relish tasty dishes. Sometimes, it even appears as if people don't eat to live but they live only to eat! In creating such a situation, the contribution of advertisements of processed food, released through different mass-media is by no means small.

The popular image of a fat person is that he is a happy-go lucky man, always jovial and gay. In fact, fat persons have little option but to project only this side of their personality. Behind the mask of his smiling face and sense of humour lies his tremendous internal conflict.

That psychological factors also play a role in causing obesity, is a well-known fact since years.

It is a popular way to try to find an easy solution to serious problems and tensions of life through food. Sense of insecurity, depression and failure generate tendency to eat more and more. Constant activity of eating gives some mental peace to a person. A fat person generally tries to develop a false sense of security by indulging in overeating. During the course of his survey of 500 fat persons, Dr. Freed[15] noticed that 370 of them were eating more when they were worried or depressed, 95 ate more when they were tired or bored; and the remaining 35 had nothing but genuine love for food and eating. Emotional excitement can be suppressed with a heavy meal. A meal is a symbol of love and affection. When a person fails in getting love from any quarters, such a love-hungry person finds a sweet alternative in food. And that is perhaps the reason why we insist on forcing our guests to eat, displaying thereby our love, warmth and affection for them!

It is also believed that spinsters, young widows and women who are deprived of conjugal happiness also tend to be fat. Obesity is common among childless couples.[16] Man can transfer and transform his happiness very tactfully. Sometimes a grave psychological shock can also generate obesity.[17]

Those who have spent their infanthood and childhood in poverty and starvation are never able to forget or drive away the fear of unsatisfied hunger. When such persons come into some more money or wealth, they tend to eat more and more. This is generally the cause of obesity among self-made men.

In short, fat people maintain their psychological balance by overeating. And gradually they form carbohydrate addiction.[18, 19]

Fat people generally present their obesity as an excuse to cover their failures and laziness. Obesity helps them in avoiding chores which they dislike or which involve any physical exertion. They make obesity a convenient excuse to avoid attending social functions or to avoid responsibilities associated with marriage and consequently with rearing a family.

Once obesity takes its roots in the body, a person begins to consider himself different from others and tends to be lonely. Such a development adds to his emotional problems. This, in turn, causes further obesity creating a vicious circle.

However, mental tension does not always lead to obesity. In some cases, the process is reverse; some people tend to eat less and less and gradually become lean due to weight-loss.

In short, psychological factors do play an important role in causing obesity. If a person fails to reduce his weight even after resorting to all the known remedies, it is likely that some psychological problem is at work behind his obesity.

(3) Endocrine gland disorders in obesity: Malfunctioning of endocrine glands is rarely a cause of obesity.

In cases of some children, Frohlich's syndrome, a disorder of the pituitary gland causes obesity. Accumulation of fat is characteristic in such cases. It generally accumulates around chest and bottoms. Genital organs of such children remain underdeveloped. However, some experts disagree with this view. They believe that pituitary gland is not responsible for this, but it is some injury to the hypothalamus which is responsible for this.

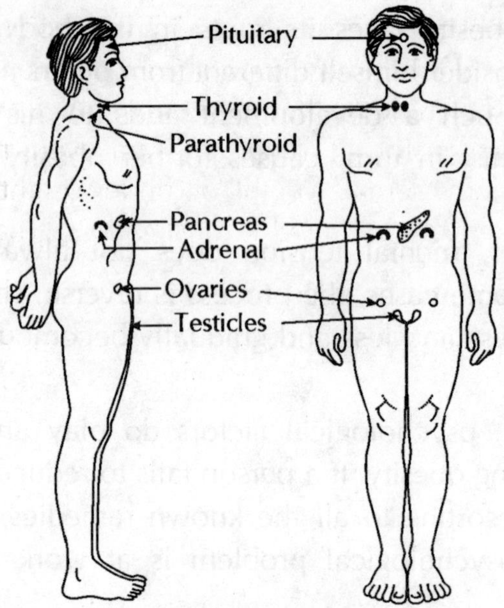

Fig. 13 : Endocrine glands and their positions

Note : For the sake of convenience, ovaries (feminine reproductive glands) are also included here.

Sometimes, inadequate secretion of thyroid gland brings down the metabolism of fat and creates obesity. However, experts are not unanimous in their opinion in this regard.

Cushing's syndrome can also sometimes cause obesity in middle aged women. In this syndrome, fat accumulates on head, trunk and around neck; while arms and legs remain thin. Less secretion of testicular hormones can also sometimes cause obesity. In cases of such men, fat accumulates on their chest, buttocks and thighs. Sometimes, in cases of women, disorders of ovarian secretions are also linked with obesity. However, it has been noticed that after some weight-loss, irregularities in menstruation cycle and infertility disappear. And that is the reason why some experts advise us to consider hormonal imbalances not as a cause but as an effect of obesity.

Relation between obesity and hyposecretion of the pancreas is very well-known. Most of the diabetic patients are obese. It is significant that by reducing their weight such patients derive a lot of relief or can even reverse the disease. In fact, normal weight or underweight is like an insurance taken out against the onslaught of diabetes.

Many experts hold a firm belief that disorders of endocrine glands do not cause obesity but obesity can cause disorders of endocrine secretions. In short, in most of the cases of obesity disorders of endocrine glands are not responsible.

(4) Lack of physical exertion and obesity: It is a universally recognized fact that fat people lack the necessary physical exertion. Many experiments have shown that when an ordinary person increases his physical activity, his food intake also goes up. But by reducing his physical exertion his food intake does not decrease correspondingly. In fact, in some cases, it appears to be increasing.

In modern society, the rate of physical exertion seems to have gone down due to social and industrial considerations. The society looks down upon those who are engaged in manual jobs, whereas those who are engaged in white-collar jobs are held in respect.

About 300 calaroies can be burnt even if a person walks only 3 miles a day. Lack of this simple exercise can add to his body one kg in a month! This fact shows how important physical exercise is in the long run.

Thus, it is imperative that those who wish to succeed in their efforts to lose excess fat have to increase their physical activities.

(5) Metabolic disorder in obesity: The question whether it is obesity that causes metabolic disorder or is it the metabolic disorder that causes obesity has been a great challenge for modern science.

There is a section of people which says, 'We eat very little, and yet our weight keeps on increasing.' While another section says, 'We don't put on weight, however much we eat and however rich food we eat.'

People can be broadly divided into two categories based on the distinction of their capacity to deal with the food consumed by them in excess to the requirement. When people of one category consume excess food, a lot of heat is generated in their body which burns the food away and consequently their weight remains constant. Dr. Richard Mackarness calls such people 'Mr. Constant Weight'. People of the other category are not able to burn away the excess food consumed by them and consequently their weight keeps on increasing. They are termed 'Mr. Fatten Easily'.

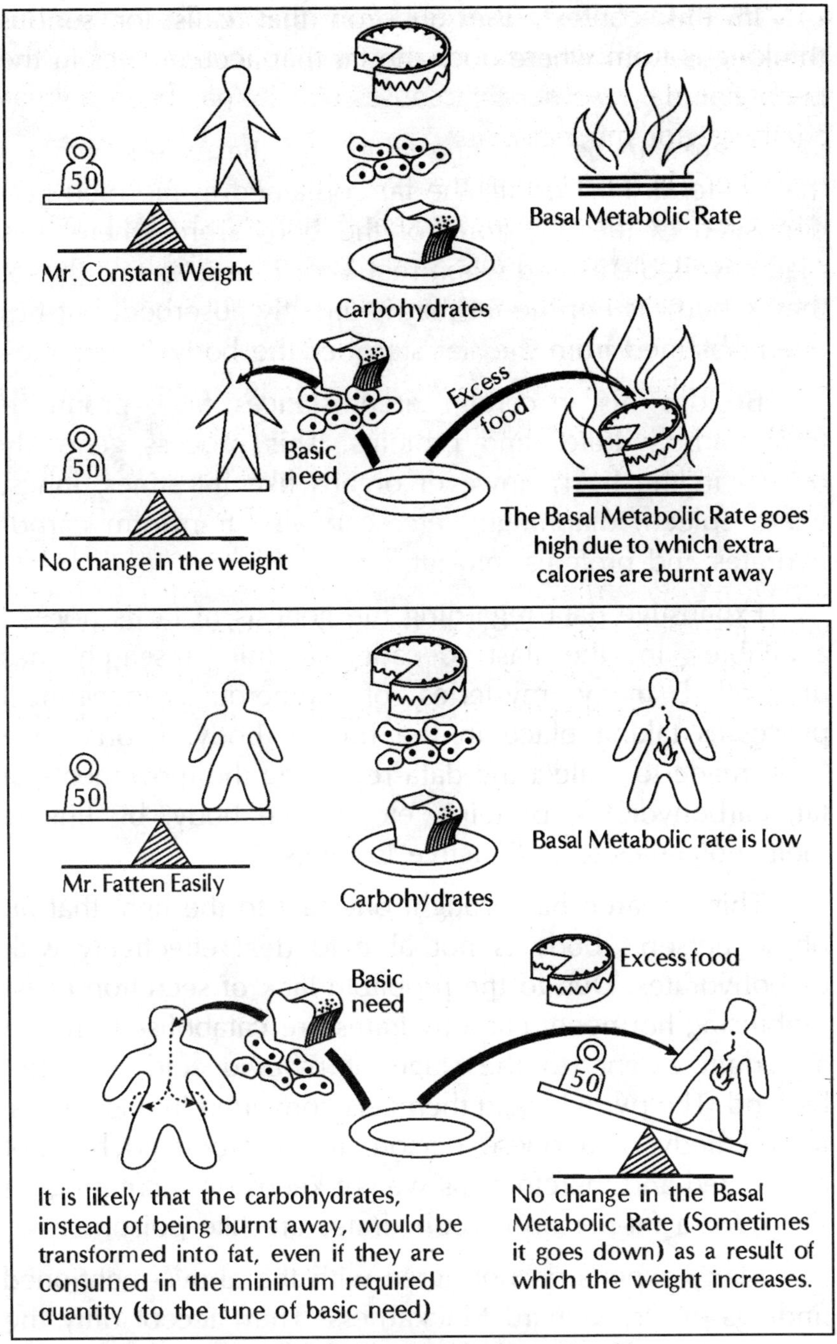

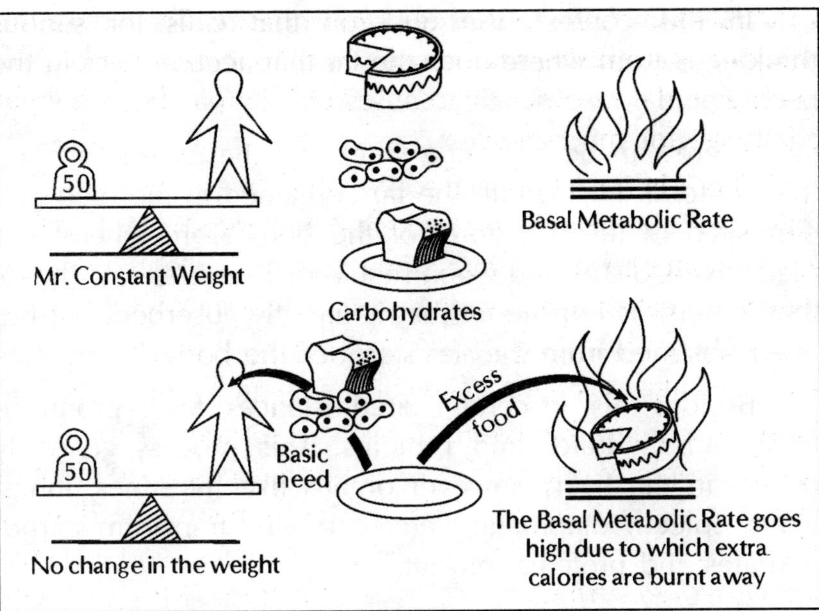

50
Mr. Constant Weight
Carbohydrates
Basal Metabolic Rate
50
Basic need
Excess food
No change in the weight
The Basal Metabolic Rate goes high due to which extra calories are burnt away
50
Mr. Fatten Easily
Carbohydrates
Basal Metabolic rate is low
Basic need
Excess food
50
It is likely that the carbohydrates, instead of being burnt away, would be transformed into fat, even if they are consumed in the minimum required quantity (to the tune of basic need)
No change in the Basal Metabolic Rate (Sometimes it goes down) as a result of which the weight increases.

Fig. 14 : Carbohydrates are the fat man's poison

In this context, the question that calls for serious thinking is from where does the fat that accumulates in the body come ?

There can be only one source of the excess fat–and that is–food. First of all, the fat contained in the food gets deposited in the 'fat store' of the body from where it is made available as and when required. That is to say, the fat that is burnt is not the fat that is directly absorbed, but has been obtained from the 'fat store' of the body.[20]

Besides this, in certain circumstances, fat is produced from carbohydrates and proteins. This process generally occurs in the liver; however organs like intestines, lungs, heart, spleen, diaphragm, etc. can also transform carbohydrates and proteins into fat.[21]

Exhaustive data regarding the genesis of fat is not yet available. In the last decade, atomic research has unravelled many mysteries of numerous biochemical processes taking place in the human body. Efforts have been made to collect the data regarding the movements of fat, carbohydrates, proteins, etc. in the body, by linking their molecules to radioactive isotopes.

This research has brought one fact to the light that an obese person's body is not able to deal effectively with carbohydrates. Due to the probable lack of secretion of fat mobilising hormone, carbohydrates are catabolised only to a certain extent (to the stage of pyruvic acid) and not beyond. The pyruvic acid then gets converted into fat. Thus, in the body of a obese person, fat is produced but not eliminated and therefore his weight keeps on increasing. In short, for a fat-person carbohydrates are like poison.

Many experts do not agree with the above-mentioned findings of Dr. Richard Mackarness. They accept only the theory of energy imbalance. According to them fat increases when a person consumes more food than required for his body.

The frequency of meals also affects the metabolism. The production of fat increases if a person eats only one meal and that too in a large quantity.[22] High levels of glucose and insulin produced in the blood have been found to be responsible for this. The production of fat rises sharply if a person takes a heavy meal late in the evening or at night. The probability of fat production goes down if instead of taking a heavy meal at a single sitting, the same quantity of food is taken in parts during the day at some intervals. In an experiment carried out on 379 men, by Dr. Fabry[23] in Prague in 1964, it was noticed that the reduction in weight was more in cases of those who were given the food five times a day and the reduction in weight was less in cases of those who were given the food three times a day, the total quantity of food being the same in both the cases.

Contradictory opinions are expressed on the issue whether there is any difference between the basal metabolic rate of the obese and the normal. Dr. Kekwick and Dr. Pawan of the Middlesex Hospital, London, have proved, through their experiments, that Mr. Constant Weight and Mr. Fatten Easily have different metabolic rates. When carbohydrates are taken in a large quantity, the metabolic rate drops, which slows down the process of burning away the food and consequently fat is produced. On the other hand, the proteins and fatty substances increase the metabolic rate, which burns away the excess food and consequently the weight of a person remains steady. Here it seems irrelevant to be dragged deeper into the controversy on the basal metabolic rate; because all the experts are unanimous on one point and it is that it is inevitable to reduce the intake of carbohydrates for reducing the excess fat.

It is but natural that here a question may arise in someone's mind that, would the basal metabolic rate not drop if the food intake is reduced? The answer to this question is that if proteins are taken in an adequate quantity, the basal metabolic rate is maintained and the accumulated fat is burnt faster.[24]

(6) Percentage of fat in men and women: Generally, in the body of an average adult young man percentage of the fat is about 7 to 8%, while it is about 15% in case of an adult young woman. With advancing age, the likelihood of women becoming obese is greater than that of men. Sometimes, the weight gained during the pregnancy does not get reduced after delivery. In cases of some women, there is a weight gain at the time of menopause and thereafter.

(7) The size of fat-depot and obesity: In the human body, fat is present in the form of an independent tissue called 'adipose tissue'. Adipose tissue contains a large number of fat cells.

During the first year of a child's life, the number of fat cells has a tendency to increase. After the age of one year, there is no appreciable change in the number of fat cells. The size of individual fat cells, however, may increase or decrease, depending upon the nature of energy imbalance.

Thus, if a child is excessively fat during the first year of his life, the number of fat cells increases rapidly. Later on, fat gets accumulated in these cells and obesity ensues.

Some other miscellaneous and uncommon reasons:

Smoking: Generally, it has been noticed that the weight of the non-smokers is slightly higher than that of the smokers. The element of nicotine in the tobacco increases the secretion of growth hormone which burns away the fat.[25] Based on their study of 10,000 Welsh steel labourers,

Dr. Khosla and Dr. Lowe hold the belief that the non-smokers aged 40 and above weigh, on an average, 5.9 kg more than the smokers.[26] It has also been found that some people gain weight after they give up smoking.[27]

Tranquilizer drugs: (A) Anti-depressant drugs: Dr. Lovrein says that a drug called Amitryptiline stops the shedding of accumulated excess fat and increases the weight.[28] According to Dr. Paykel, this drug increases carbohydrate craving.[29] Dr. Wendsburgh has proved that another drug–Lithium–makes a person thirsty very frequently and eventually this results in weight gain.

(B) Sleep-inducing drugs: Prolonged use of chlorpromazine causes weight gain.[30] Proclorparazine and other drugs of Phynothiazine group also produce a similar effect.

Pregnancy: Some weight-gain during pregnancy is a natural development. Chapter 23 contains a detailed discussion on this topic.

Sometimes, there may be a sudden weight gain in patients suffering from diseases like diabetes, cancer or kidney diseases.

It should be borne in mind that any one of the causes discussed above is never solely responsible for causing obesity. It is the energy imbalance (input and output of calories in the body) which is responsible for manifestation of obesity and more than one of the above-mentioned causes are jointly responsible for causing this imbalance. There can be reduction in weight only if the two processes occur simultaneously–i.e., the body should get less amount of calories and should spend them more.

Synopsis:

1. Overeating and lack of physical activity are the main causes of obesity.
2. Genetic factors are also partly responsible for causing obesity.
3. Malfunctioning of endocrine glands is generally not responsible for causing obesity.
4. Basal metabolic rate is generally slow in a fat person's body and therefore the excess food is not burnt away, which eventually results in production of fat. For fat persons, carbohydrates are their greatest enemy.
5. If a child is given excess food in the first year of his life, it increases the number of fat cells in his body which later on makes him obese.

References:

1. Hodges, R. E. & Krehl, W. A. (1965)–The role of carbohydrates in lipid metabolism, *Am. J. Clin. Nutr.,* 17, 334.
2. Chang, C. A., Mckenna. R. D. & Beck, I. T. (1968)–Gastric emptying rate of the water and fat phases of a mixed test meal in man. *Gut.* 9,420.
3. Mayer, J. (1953)–Genetic traumatic and environmental factors in the aetiology of obesity, *Physiol. Rev.* 33, 472.
4. Brobeck J. R. (1948)–Food intake as a mechanism of temperature regulation, *Yale J. Biol Med.,* 20, 545.
5. Strang, J. M. & McCluggage, H. B. (1931)–The specific dynamic action of food in abnormal states of nutrition: *Am. J. M. Sc.,* 182, 49.
6. Gurney, R. (1936)–The hereditory factor in obesity, *Arch. Int. Med.,* 51:557
7. Evans, F. (1942)–In *Diseases of Metabolism,* edited by Garfield Duncan, W. B. Saunders Co., Philadelphia.
8. Newman, H. H. et al (1937)–*Twins, A Study of Heredity and Environment,* University of Chicago Press, Chicago.
9. Shields, J. (1962)–*Monozygotic twins brought up apart and brought up together,* Oxford University Press, London.
10. Withers, R. F. J. (1964)–Problems in genetics of human obesity, *Eugen. Rev.,* 56.81.
11. Mall, G. (1947)–Quoted by American Academy of Paediatrics, Committee on Nutrition (1967). Obesity in childhood. *Paediatrics,* Springfield, 40, 455.
12. Marston. A. R. et al (1975)–*Recent advances in obesity research,* ed. Howarth A. P., 207, Newman, London.

13. Woolley, O. W. et al (1975)–*Recent advances in obesity research,* 212, Newman, London.

14. Rynearson, E. H. & Gastineau, C. W. (1949)–*Obesity,* Springfield, Ill., Chas. C. Thomas, Publishers.

15. Freed, S. C. (1947)–Factors in the development and treatment of obesity, *J. A. M. A.,* 133, 369.

16. Dennis Craddock (1978)–*Obesity and its management,* 3rd edition, Churchill Livingston, New York.

17. Bruch, H. (1940)–Physiologic and Psychologic aspects of food intake of obese children, *Am. J. Dis. Childh.,* 59, 739.

18. Bloom, W. L. & Clarke, M. B. (1964)–The Obese Carboholic, *J. Obesity,* 1, 10.

19. Hamburgher, W. W. (1951)–Emotional aspect of Obesity. *Med. Clins. N. Am.* 35, 483.

20. Schoenheimer, R. & Rittenburg, D. (1935)–Deuterium as an indicator in the study of intermediary metabolism. III. The role of fat tissues, *J. Biol. Chem.* III:175.

21. Popjak, G. & Beekman, M. L. (1950)–Extrahepatic lipid synthesis, *Biochem. J.,* 47 : 233.

22. Bray, G. A. (1969)–Effects of caloric restriction on energy expenditure in obese patients. *Lancet. ii,* 397.

23. Fabry, P. et al (1964)–The frequency of meals : its relation to overweight, hypercholesterolaemia and decreased glucose tolerance, *Lancet,* ii, 614.

24. Rynearson, E. H. & Gastineau, C. W. (1949)–*Obesity,* Springfield, Ill., Chas. C. Thomas, Publishers.

25. Sandberg, H. et al (1973)–The effect of smoking on serum somatotrophins in young adult males, *J. Pharmac. and Exp. Therap.,* 184, 787.

26. Khosla, T. and Lowe, C. R. (1971)–Obesity and smoking habits, *Br. med. J.* iv, 10.

27. Glaiser, S. C. et al (1970)–Metabolic changes associated with the omission of cigarette smoking. *Arch Environmental H.,* 20, 337.

28. Lovrien, F. C. et al (1972)–Effect of Amitryptiline on lipolysis and cyclic AMP concentration in isolated fat cells, *Metabolism,* 21, 223.

29. Paykel, E. S. et al (1973)–Amitryptiline weight gain and carbohydrate craving:a side effect. *Brit j. Psychiat.,* 123, 501.

30. Clark, M. et al (1970)-The effect of chlorpromazine on serum cholesterol in chronic schizophrenic patients. *Clin. Pharm.* 11, 883.

FROM FAT TO FIT

SECTION 2

Treatment of obesity

6. PREVENTION OF OBESITY

The old adage – Prevention is better than cure – is equally applicable to the disease of obesity also. The prevention of obesity is extraordinarily important if we take into account the hazards and disadvantages associated with it.

(1) Proper education of pregnant women : Generally women develop health awareness during pregnancy. If proper habits of eating and living are developed during this period, it is likely that they may continue for lifetime. And besides that afterwards their children may also imbibe them. Those babies who develop correct habits in their childhood are saved from obesity in their later life.

(2) Breast-feeding : For a child, breast-feeding is like an insurance policy against obesity. Several experiments show that breast-fed babies are less obese than those fed on external milk.

(3) Diet-control during the first year of infant's life : Generally the fat in the human body is in the form of independent adipose tissues. Usually fat cells are formed during the first year of an infant's life, and their number does not increase afterwards. So, if an infant is overfed during the first year of its life, the number of fat cells exceeds the normal limit. Later on, fat gets deposited in these cells, eventually causing obesity. In other words, if the number of fat cells is not allowed to exceed normal limits, the chances of developing obesity are also reduced.

The infant would remain grateful to you forever if you look after its health and diet during the first year of its life.

(4) Control over carbohydrate intake : It is an undisputed fact that large intake of carbohydrates plays a crucial role in causing obesity. In modern times, it is becoming a common practice that when a child is about three months old parents start giving him grains and other carbohydrates instead of milk. It is imperative that this trend should be reversed. If an infant is not overfed with carbohydrates during the first year of his life, the possibility of his becoming obese later on are reduced almost to nil[2]. In short, do not let the child develop carbohydrate addiction. Right from the beginning, encourage him to cultivate the habit of taking proper and balanced diet. There is no need to harbour the fear that a slim child will be a weak child. That a rotund child is a healthy one is a common illusion.

(5) **Chew the food properly:** Always insist that your child should chew his food properly. Such eating habits are best cultivated during infancy only. The food should not be so soft that the child can gulp it down his throat without making any effort to chew it.

(6) **Encourage physical activity:** Sometimes, fond parents pamper their children and don't let them participate in sports or other physical activities. They are always afraid that their child will be hurt if he indulges in any such activity. This overprotective attitude of parents harms the child in the long run. Lack of physical activity makes the child plump and later on he too turns to reading or indoor games for his recreation.

(7) **Create proper environment for the child:** Earlier, we have discussed how important are psychological factors in causing obesity. It is likely that those children who do not experience enough sense of safety and security in the house or are deprived of parental attention and affection seek to compensate this loss through overeating. So, the parents should pay careful attention to fulfil not only the physical needs of the child but also the psychological needs.

In some homes, the marital life of the parents is not a happy one. The atmosphere in such homes is generally disturbed and charged with mutual hatred. It lacks the essential qualities like love, warmth and compassion which make the child happy. Such a child seeks solace in eating. Dr. Irwin holds a firm belief that those parents who wish that their child should not become obese, should create in their home an atmosphere of mutual goodwill.

Synopsis:

1. Obesity can easily be prevented by taking appropriate timely measures.
2. Development of obesity can be prevented by cultivating proper eating habits during pregnancy, by breast-feeding a child, by controlling the intake of carbohydrate foods in small children and by encouraging physical activity.

References:

1. Denis Craddock (1978)–*Obesity and its management,* p. 179, Churchill Livingston, New York.
2. Hooper, P. D. (1973)–Infantile overnutrition. *Br. Med. J.,* iii. 237.

7. AN IMPORTANT QUESTIONNAIRE

It is an established fact that the person who has acquired proper understanding of the causes responsible for his obesity can lose his excess weight more easily and effectively.

Sometimes, psychological dilemmas also hamper a person's efforts for reducing his weight. In such cases, his reasoning tells him to reduce, but his conscience resists this move. If a person becomes aware of this psychological factor operating behind his obesity, his efforts to reduce obesity meet with success. Keeping this fact in mind, we have prepared a questionnaire. Readers are advised to give full and frank answers to these questions.

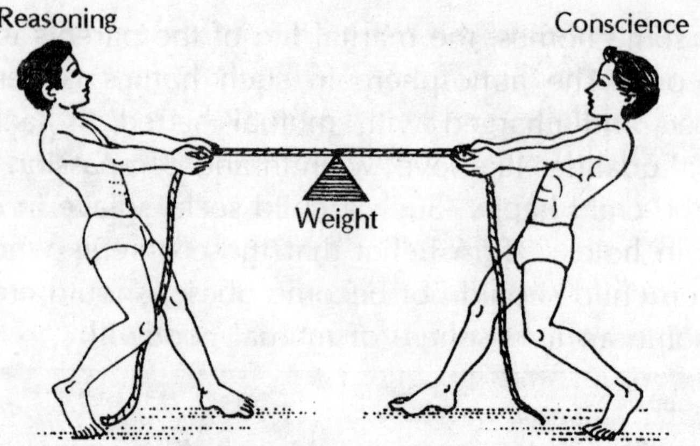

Fig. 15 : Conflict between reasoning and conscience

(A) 1. Why do you wish to reduce your weight? ....

2. Are you ashamed of your looks? ....

3. Do you get breathless while doing common household chores? ....

4. Have you started suffering from any chronic illness? ....

5. Does obesity bother you in any other way? Which? ....

(B) Do you have any family history of diabetes, heart disease or high blood pressure? ....

(C) 1. How many times do you eat during a day? ....

2. How many times do you take full meals? ....

3. Do you eat between the two meals? ....

4. Do you like sweet dishes? ....

5. Do you drink alcohol? ....

(D) 1. Do you eat when you are in a disturbed mental state? ....

2. Do you eat more when you are depressed or unhappy? ....

(E) 1. Are you happy? ....
2. How much? average, very much or absolutely? ....
3. Were you happy during your childhood? ....
4. Have you ever broken down mentally? ....
5. Are you, at present, surrounded by worries and anxieties? ....
6. Is your life stable? ....

(F) Only for women:
1. Are you married? ....
2. Are you afraid of the married life? ....
3. Were you married at the proper age? ....
4. Are you happy by your present marriage? ....
5. Do you have any children? ....

(G) Only for men:
1. How do you commute to your place of work? on foot/by bus or train/by your own vehicle? ....
2. Do you have a sedentary job? ....
3. How many miles do you walk everyday on an average? ....
4. Do you feel tired in the evening? ....
5. Do you have any hobbies? ....

(H) Only for women:
1. Do you do all the household chores yourself? ....
2. Do you go for shopping personally? ....

(I) 1. Do you take any medicines regularly? ....
2. Are they barbiturates? ....
3. Are they tranquillizers? ....
4. Are they sleep-inducing drugs? ....

(J) What weight would you prefer to have? ....

Note: Proceed further only after you have replied to all the questions fully and frankly.

8. PRINCIPLES OF DIETING

Food intake generates and conserves energy in the body. This energy is then spent when a person is engaged in daily routine or in some hard work. In the body of a healthy person, this balance between energy generation and energy expenditure is properly maintained and consequently his weight remains steady.

Same is not the case with the body of an obese person. In his body, the energy expenditure is less than the energy generation. This upsets the balance between the two, eventually causing obesity. The basic principle underlying all the efforts to reduce excess fat is to reverse this imbalance. One of the most important remedial measures in this direction is–dieting.

Before we discuss dieting, it would be useful to acquire some elementary information about various ingredients of our routine diet.

The human body needs energy in order to make movements of limbs and activate internal organs. This energy is derived from the food. Just as metre is a measure of length and gram is a measure of weight, calorie is a measure of energy contained in the food-stuff.

As defined in physics, 'Calorie is that amount of heat which is required to raise the temperature of one gram of water by one degree celsius.' Just as heat is generated when wood or coal is burnt, similarly when the food is burnt in the body, heat is generated. Different individuals need different amounts of calories. If a person has to work hard, he needs more calories.

The following are some of the chief components of our routine diet:

Carbohydrates, fats, proteins, vitamins and minerals.

It has been discovered through a study that one gram of fat supplies nine calories to the body; and one gram of carbohydrates or one gram of proteins supply four calories to the body.

Though true, the above figures are slightly misleading. Our experience and some other experiments indicate that owing to their inherent, high specific dynamic action, proteins generate more heat than shown above. It has also been noticed that the carbohydrates have the lowest S.D.A. (specific dynamic action).

Given below is brief information regarding some of the chief components of our routine diet.

Carbohydrates: Carbohydrates are known as the fuel of the body-furnace. They are available in two forms: sugar and starch. Their only function is to generate heat in the body. They are lacking in all the other nutrients that are required for the nourishment of the body. There is always a possibility of excess consumption of carbohydrates as they are cheap and easily available. When the food intake is in excess, coupled with the lack of physical activity, the circumstances conducive to obesity are created.

Excess consumption of carbohydrates creates malnutrition. This in turn creates a craving for food, and carbohydrates are always at hand to satisfy this craving. But that doesn't remove malnutrition. A vicious cycle is thus established. The low specific dynamic action of the carbohydrates is actually responsible for developing repeated craving for food in case of those who subsist mainly on carbohydrates.

As discussed earlier, the metabolism of a fat person is not able to deal properly with the carbohydrates which are not therefore burnt away fully. The residue gets deposited as fat in the body. Carbohydrates are, thus, the greatest enemy of a fat person.

Grains, edible roots, sugar, jaggery and some fruits like banana are carbohydrate foods.

Proteins: Proteins are substances that build our body. They contain an important element called nitrogen. For maintaining the health and the efficiency of the body nitrogen balance is very essential. Without protein the body cannot produce the necessary enzymes and hormones for the exchange of energy.

The importance of proteins lies in their high specific dynamic action. They expedite the metabolism which in turn burns away that food which is in excess of actual requirements. This high specific dynamic action of the protein controls the excess appetite and curbs the tendency to eat frequently. This is a very important and welcome development for a fat person. Protein also plays an important role in draining away the excess fluid from the body. In short, for a fat person, if the carbohydrates are like a poison, the proteins are like nectar. According to Dr. Richard Mackarness, obesity is an indication of protein deficiency in the body.

Based on the distinction of its sources, the protein is divided into two categories: vegetable protein and animal protein. Each of them has its own distinct advantages and disadvantages. Generally, the animal protein is considered to be of superior quality. However, vegetable protein of a similar first-class quality can be produced by proper mixing of some pulses.

Milk, buttermilk, curd, pulses, cereals, etc. are some of the sources of vegetable proteins. Sources of animal proteins are fish, meat, eggs, etc.

Fats: Fats too perform the function of generating heat and energy in the body. Whenever excess food is consumed, it is transformed into fat and gets deposited. Fat is, thus, the accumulated or stored energy in the body, which can afterwards be utilized as and when required. The fats protect the body against cold. They fill up all the vacant spaces between the body-cells and make the movements of the joints smooth by lubricating them. They are an essential ingredient for the human body.

Vitamins 'A', 'D', 'E' and 'K' are soluble only in the fats. These vitamins are absorbed in the body only after they are synthesised in the fats[1]. If the diet does not contain adequate quantity of fats, diseases caused by the deficiency of the above-mentioned vitamins may develop.[2]

Butter, ghee, oil, some grains and animal flesh are some of the chief sources of fat.

Vitamins: Vitamins are organic substances necessary, albeit in small quantities, for perfect health, peak efficiency and optimum metabolism in the body. But on its own, the body is incapable of manufacturing them.

Vitamins are essential for growth, for formation of bones and teeth, for vigour, for proper functioning of various internal organs and for longer life. Vitamins also supply the body with vitality and resistance power against disease. Diseases like beriberi, scurvy, rickets, etc. are caused by vitamin deficiencies.

Heating or cooking, more or less destroy vitamins and therefore it is advisable to eat raw vegetables and uncooked food.

Sources of different vitamins, their functions in the body and diseases caused by their deficiency are described in the table given in the appendix 3 at the end of the book.

Minerals: Minerals too are as important as vitamins for the human body. They are essential for various purposes such as, for smooth functioning of various systems in the body, for the muscle tone, for maintaining regular heartbeats, for the free movement of blood and fluids in the cells, for maintaining the balance between acids and antacids in the body and for a host of other important functions.

If minerals are missing from a person's diet, he can't survive beyond a fortnight or so. Mineral-free diet causes a person's death quicker than even the total starvation does.[3]

Of the many minerals, calcium, phosphorus, potassium, sodium, iron, magnesium, chlorine and iodine are more important for our body. At the end of the book, in appendix 4, you'll find details about the sources of minerals, their functions and diseases caused by their deficiency.

Slimming diet: Diet for slimming should be so planned that the following three aims are fulfilled:

(1) The weight should get reduced: For reducing weight, a person should take such diet which contains less number of calories than spent by him everyday. The actual number of calories to be consumed depends upon the fact how fast a person wishes to reduce his weight. The amount of calories may be reduced gradually and safely. Dr. Strang, Dr. McCluggage and Dr. Evans say that there would be no problem even if a person were allowed a diet of 444 calories only and containing 0.9 gram protein per every kg of the ideal body weight. Those patients who were kept on such a diet on experimental basis appeared to be in a happy mood, felt fit and the nitrogen balance in their body was also maintained. In spite of losing 21 kgs weight in 100 days, these patients did not show any signs of ketosis[4]. In his book 'Principles & Practice of Medicine', Davidson says that many patients had remained in quite a healthy state though they were given the food containing just 400 calories and were made to take an exercise of walking for 10 miles everyday. If adequate quanities of vitamins and minerals are administered parenterally, no harm is done to the health of a heavily overweight patient even if he is made to fast for a number of days. It is true that prolonged fasting may sometimes cause ketosis. But some experts believe that even this development is a blessing in disguise as it expedites the process of burning away the excess fat[5]. However, such an experiment of drastic calorie-control should be carried out only at a hospital or under proper medical supervision. For ordinarily fat people, such a drastic measure is not desirable. In this book, you will find a separate chapter on the advantages and disadvantages of fasting for removing obesity.

(2) The body should get all the necessary ingredients in adequate quantities: Besides the number of calories contained in food, the following points should also be borne in mind:

The body should get everyday, about 1 gm of proteins per kg of the ideal weight.

Some carbohydrates should also be included in the diet to supplement the proteins and prevent ketosis.

Care should also be taken to maintain the adequate quantity of vitamins and minerals. If their deficiency develops, they can be administered parenterally.

(3) Diet should be conducive to cultivating proper eating habits: The diet should be such that the patient would take it happily and would not form aversion to it. If the diet is not to the taste of the patient, the treatment won't last long.

Cultivating proper eating habits is equally important, because after all, faulty eating habits are the root cause of obesity. The real aim of treatment is not only to reduce weight but also to maintain the reduction thereafter.

Plan for a slimming diet:

(1) Proteins: Diet should be so planned that the body gets about 50 to 60 grams of proteins everyday. This much quantity of proteins is necessary for maintaining the nitrogen balance in the body. Some dieticians recommend a high-protein diet. According to them, we should avail of the high S.D.A. of the protein. It is true that S.D.A. of the protein is five times more than that of the carbohydrates. However, it is almost impossible to obtain foodstuffs containing only protein. Generally proteins and carbohydrates are available only in the combined form and the effective S.D.A. of the food in which they are combined is far less.

By subsisting only on the proteins, calories to the tune of 150 can be reduced from the daily diet; but this advantage of reduction in the calories is set off by the disadvantages caused by the protein-rich diet. High-protein diet is essentially unnatural. After a few days, the tongue proclaims a rebellion against it. This problem remains unsolved even if a patient has a strong will-power or is able to ignore the unpleasant taste. What happens after reducing the weight and bringing it to the desirable level with the help of such a diet? An unnatural diet cannot be taken throughout the life. Besides, losing weight is only a part of the total treatment. Maintaining the weight-loss is equally important. After bringing the weight down to a desirable level, if one has to cultivate correct dietary habits of balanced food, why not, in the first instance, bring the weight down through a balanced diet? This is a very important point and calls for serious thinking.

Protein powder: As a part of some slimming programmes, patients are given protein powders. They are either to be sprinkled on the food or taken as a substitute of the food. While doing this, it is hoped that the S.D.A. of protein would burn away the excess fat. However, as discussed earlier this S.D.A. does not yield the expected big gain.

Dr. Gelvin[6] carried out an experiment on two groups of patients. One group was recommended to take a balanced diet of 1200 calories. The other group was advised to take protein powder as a substitute for some portion of the food. Care was taken to ensure that in either case the total calories did not exceed 1200. After two months, when the patients were examined, following findings emerged:

	Balanced diet of 1200 calories	Balanced diet of 1200 calories (inclusive of protein powder)
Number of patients	15	13
Duration of the experiment	8 weeks	8 weeks
Average weight-loss every week	0.9 pounds	1.2 pounds
Side effects	0	38 %

In short, there was not much of a difference in the rate of weight reduction in case of the two groups; but many patients who were advised to take protein powder complained of nausea, vomitting, constipation and burning sensation in the stomach.

Thus, the rate of weight-loss can be increased by taking protein powder; but due to its side effects, it is advisable to start taking it only under medical supervision.

(2) Carbohydrates: It is an undisputable fact that those who wish to reduce their weight should drastically cut down carbohydrates from their diet. In reality, it is the consumption of these carbohydrates which is the real culprit causing obesity. In a food containing 1000 calories, the proportion of carbohydrates should not exceed 100 grammes. It is essential to stop the use of sugar totally as it contains no nutritional value. It does not create any feeling of satiety and creates false hunger.

There is not a grain of truth in the argument that a cut in carbohydrates causes ketosis. It is an unfair tendency to hold ketosis responsible for the initial troubles during dieting such as headache, weakness or nausea of some patients.

In some exceptional cases, symptoms of hypoglycaemia appear due to low carbohydrate diet. These symptoms include uneasiness, tension, perspiration, delirium, lunacy or unconsciousness. It is the previous high carbohydrate diet intake that raises the level of insulin in their blood and consequently causes these developments. Such patients should decrease their carbohydrate intake gradually to avoid these symptoms.

(3) Fats: In a diet containing 100 grams of carbohydrates and 50 to 60 grams of protein, the proportion of fat should not exceed 40 to 50 grams. Though small, this proportion of fat is adequate for the body.

There are some experts who recommend that this proportion of the fat should be raised and the proportion of the carbohydrates should be reduced. The slogan raised by them is: 'Eat fat & grow slim'. Dr. Pennington[7] is one of the leading exponents of this theory. Giving a scientific explanation to support his theory, he says that the metabolism (process of burning) of carbohydrates in the body takes place in a number of ways. In a fat person's body carbohydrates are not burnt away completely due to a peculiar defect of digestive system. The metabolism of carbohydrates stops after it reaches the stage of pyruvic acid. This pyruvic acid accumulates in the body and hampers the reduction of fat. This problem can be solved by reducing the carbohydrate intake. Moreover, mild ketosis is caused by increasing the fat intake. Ketosis, at first, separates the fat from the tissues and then eliminates it. The fat is thus reduced from the body.

In spite of these arguments, 'the high-fat diet' is not above suspicion. Like 'high protein diet' this diet is also unnatural and patients can't put up with it for a long time. It is a well-known fact that in the long run fat-rich diet can create hazardous consequences for the body in general and the heart and blood-vessels in particular.

Dr. Pilkington,[8] Dr. Oleson and Dr. Quaade say that the initial weight-loss that occurs after putting the patient on a fat-rich diet is illusive, as it is mainly a result of elimination of water and fluids from the body. If a patient deviates from this diet programme even once and takes carbohydrates, his weight suddenly jacks up. Besides that, the argument about the balanced diet that was presented during the course of the discussion on the protein is equally applicable here.

(4) Vitamins: During the period of dieting, the food should contain plenty of raw vegetables and fruits. The body gets adequate quantity of vitamins and minerals from them. Vegetables contain low calories and yet they fill up the stomach and give the feeling of satiety. Thereafter the person does not feel hungry for sometime. Moreover, fibres contained in the vegetables and fruits prevent and remove constipation. Vitamin deficiency does not occur if a person continues to take adequate quantity of milk and sprouted wheat. However, if the need arises, vitamins can be taken in the synthetic form also.

(5) Minerals: Among the various minerals, calcium and iron are more important. Milk supplies us with the necessary calcium and green leafy vegetables supply the iron. If the need be, iron can be taken in the synthetic form (in the form of pills). If the symptoms of anaemia develop, more iron should be taken.

(6) Water and salt: There was a time when fat persons were advised to drink less amount of water. But scientific research has now shown that there is no logical reason for doing so. But fat persons should certainly avoid sweet drinks and soft drinks.

There is no need to pay undue attention to the maintenance of water level in the body. For that it is desirable to trust different systems functioning in the body. As shown earlier, fat persons perspire profusely and consequently they feel a bit more thirsty. There is no reason why this thirst should not be quenched.

Similarly, if a fat person is not suffering from high-blood pressure or gradual congestive cardiac failure, he need not stop consuming salt altogether. If the heart and the kidneys are functioning properly, excess water and salt are automatically eliminated from the body. However, excess consumption of salt, for making the food tastier, is not at all desirable. It must be borne in mind that one gram of salt is responsible for retention of 60 grams water in the body.

Dr. Newburgh has shown through his research that the water and the salt level may cause variations in the day to day weight, but they don't have any long-ranging effect on the weight.

Synopsis:

1. Weight-loss occurs only when the expenditure of calories (energy) exceeds the intake of calories.
2. Dieting is the most effective remedial measure for losing weight.
3. Diet should be so planned that:
   —There is reduction in weight.
   —The body is not deprived of any of the essential nutrients.
   —Proper eating habits are cultivated.
4. Slimming diet should be so planned that the body continues to get everyday about 50 to 60 gm of protein, about 100 gm of carbohydrates and about 40 to 50 gm of fat. Besides this, adequate supply of vitamins and minerals should be obtained from fruits, raw vegetables, sprouted wheat and sprouted pulses.

References:

1. Lucins Nicholls (1951)–*Tropical Nutrition and Dietetics,* p. 8, London.
2. W. M. Frazer (1953)–*Textbook of Public Health,* p. 232, London.
3. Chopra, R. N. (1936)–*A Handbook of Tropical Therapeutics,* p. 154, Kolkata.
4. Strang, J. M., McCluggage, H. B. and Evans, F. A. (1931)–The nitrogen balance during dietary correction of obesity, *Am. J. M. Sc.,* 179:678.
5. Richard Mackarness (1970)–*Eat fat and grow slim,* Pocket Books, New York.
6. Gelvin, E. P. & Thomas McGavack (1957)–*Obesity-Its cause, classification and care,* Hoeber-Harper Publishers, New York.
7. Pennington, A. W. (1953)–Practical reducing regimen, In *'overeating, overweight and obesity';* Nutrition symposium series no.6, The National Vitamin Foundation Inc. New York.
8. Pilkington, T. R. et al (1960)–Diet and weight reduction in the obese. *Lancet,* I, 856.

9. DAILY DIET-PLAN

Those who wish to reduce their weight expect some sort of guidance for their day to day diet.

In principle, they should take, a low-carbohydrate, medium-fat and high-protein diet.

It is a difficult proposition to prescribe a high-protein and low-carbohydrate diet for the vegetarians as almost all the vegetarian foods contain proteins and carbohydrates in almost equal proportions.

Those who are not seriously overweight (i.e. not weighing more than 20% than the ideal weight) need not count the calories and bother themselves with all the calculations. For them, it would suffice if they were to choose proper diet for themselves. Given below are the lists of those food items which are forbidden and those which can be taken freely by the vegetarians and the non-vegetarians.

Following items can be consumed freely in any desired quantity:

(1) Vegetables and green salads (especially containing tomatoes and cucumbers)

(2) Fresh fruits (except banana)

Following items can be taken in a limited quantity:

(1) Milk (250 ml or half a bottle or one and a half cupful). This is the quota for the whole day and includes the milk taken in tea or coffee.

(2) Butter, ghee, oil or cream-2 to 3 small tea-spoonfuls. (Some experts advise to stop taking them altogether.)

(3) Three to four chapatis (without applying ghee on them) per day.

OR

Three to four slices of bread

OR

Three to four khakharas (without applying ghee on them)

OR

1 to 2 oz (i.e., half to one small bowlful) rice or khichari

(Note: Brown bread and chapatis made from bran-rich wheat flour are preferable.)

(4) One small bowlful dal or moong soup during the whole day.

(5) One or two small potatoes during the whole day.

(6) Eggs

(7) Fish

(8) Meat

Barring the above-mentioned items no other food should be taken.

List of forbidden foods:

Biscuits, cakes, etc.

Ice cream

Sugar, chocolate, peppermint, sweets, jam, honey, etc.

Fruit-juices

Alcohol

All other grains and pulses barring those mentioned above.

Those who are severely overweight (i.e. weighing 20% more than the ideal weight) need to exercise a stricter control on their diet. The body does not need more than 800 to 900 calories per day in case of those who lead a sendantary life or 1,000 to 1,200 calories per day in case of those who are engaged in manual jobs. Consult the appendices given at the end of the book to ascertain the calorific values of various food items consumed in your day to day diet.

Given below is a model diet-plan supplying about 1,000 calories during the course of a day:

(1) Early morning: One glass of water with lemon or lime juice.

(2) Morning breakfast: Any one or two items from the list given below:

(a) 3/4 cup of milk without adding sugar or one cup of tea or coffee with a little milk. In tea or coffee saccharin, and not sugar, may be used.

(b) An orange or a mosambi or any other fruit (except banana) of an ordinary size.

(c) One slice of bread or one small khakhara. Those who are heavily overweight should avoid them.

(d) One egg (for non-vegetarians)

(e) 2 to 3 small tomatoes or cucumbers

(3) Mid-day meal :

(a) Take a cup of vegetable soup or any other soup before starting the meal.

(b) Before other courses are taken, take green-salad containing 4 to 5 tomatoes or 2 to 3 medium size cucumbers. Chew them well. These can be taken in a larger quantity also.

(c) One small bowlful of a low calorie cooked vegetable from the list given below: Green leaf bhaji, carrots, cucumber, unripe tomatoes, brinjals, cabbage, beet, radish, white gourd, French-beans, bhindi, parval, tindola, etc.

(d) One or two small chapatis or bread slices.

(e) One small cupful of moong soup or any other soup made from a common pulse or cereal.

(f) Some meat or fish for non-vegetarians.

(4) Afternoon/Early evening: As per the morning breakfast.

(5) Supper: Same as the mid-day meal. But a small cupful rice or Khichari can be taken as a substitute for bread or chapati.

Note: Some people harbour a notion that one has to starve himself in order to reduce weight. But this is a false notion. It is not the quantity but the quality or the type of food that is important. One can fill his belly by eating large quantities of low-calorie foods especially vegetables like radish, cucumber or tomatoes.

Anybody who follows the above-mentioned diet pattern can hope to reduce about 5 to 12 pound (2 to 5 kg) of weight in about a month's time. If the rate of weight-loss is less than this, it means a further reduction in quantity of the food intake is required. See Appendix 6 for diet-plans that provide 600, 800 and 1,200 calories to the body per day.

Note: In Appendix 5, there is a list of foods which can be used as substitutes for some other food items.

10. EXERCISE TO REDUCE WEIGHT

Those who are engaged in manual jobs are rarely obese. In most of the cases, obesity is the result of a sedentary life.

Many persons, particularly men, start becoming obese when they give up their regular exercise. It is noticed in our country that when a young man launches his professional career, his weight starts increasing. Before taking up a job, he usually participates in various sports or keeps moving around. But once he is harnessed in the routine, he stops all these physical activities. Almost every one of us must have come across at least one obese friend dropping a remark like this : 'I'll have to resume my early morning jogging or running.' On the other hand, those who are economically backward or are engaged in manual jobs rarely become fat.[1, 2]

In this way, the lack of physical activity makes a vital contribution to causing obesity. But whether the exercise is helpful in reducing the excess fat or not, has become a debatable issue. Those who are against the exercise base their arguments on the following points:

(1) Exercise stimulates the digestive system and makes a person more hungry. A fat person eats more after he has done the exercise and consequently this excess food intake hampers his weight-reduction process.

(2) If the weight is reduced by doing exercises, why do the wrestlers and the athletes appear fat?

(3) A fat person becomes breathless at the slightest physical exertion. His heart, respiratory system and other organs are already saddled with a heavy burden. Under such circumstances how could we add to his burden by advising him to do exercises?

In the wake of these arguments, the issue of the usefulness of the exercise in the treatment of obesity acquires a lot of importance.

First of all, the relation between physical exertion and hunger calls for a thorough examination. Dr. Mayor and his colleagues[3] have carried out numerous experiments to study the relationship between hunger and physical exertion. Their experiments have shown that if an ordinary person exerts himself, his food intake increases to a certain extent. But If he does less than normal physical activity, his food intake does not decrease (In some cases it actually increases). On the other hand, the food intake decreases after a session of heavy exercise. According to

Dr. Bjorntorp[4] exercise never stimulates a fat person's hunger. On the contrary, it causes some loss of appetite.

The argument that 'the fat you lose by doing the exercise is regained, with interest, by overeating', is nothing more than sheer self-deception on the part of that individual who wishes to resort to such logic in order to hide his weakness and laziness.

We need not be afraid of the above-mentioned argument,even if we were to accept it for the time being. The question how much do you eat is less important than the question–what items do you eat. You can easily satisfy your increased hunger by taking large quantities of a low-calorie diet.

It is true that the very reference of a wrestler creates, before our mind's eye, an image of a huge, pot-bellied obese figure. However, the argument that the exercise is the cause of a wrestler's obesity is far from the truth. In fact, such wrestlers live only to eat. Sweets, rich food, milk, cream, dry fruits and other high-calorie foodstuffs are the root causes of their obesity.

Quoting certain references from books on human physiology, some people argue that one has to walk about 36 miles a day at normal pace to reduce only 1 kg from the accumulated fat! But mind you, who advises you to walk 36 miles everyday? You don't have to reduce 1 kg everyday. You can reduce 10 pounds in a year by cycling for 45 minutes, or by swimming for 30 minutes everyday. Similarly, you can reduce your excess fat by regularly participating in any moderate physical activity or sports over a long period. In short, though the exercise may not show any short-term gains, it certainly yields invaluable longterm gains. In 1960, an experiment was conducted by Dr. Keys in London. In this experiment the weight of every participant was reduced by the exercise alone.

Given below are the findings of that experiment:

Weight before starting the exercises		Reduction in the weight due to exercise					
		at the end of the first month		at the end of the second month		at the end of the third month	
in kg	in pounds	in kg	in pounds	in kg	in pounds	in kg	in pounds
59	130	1.0	1.1	2.0	4.4	2.9	6.5
66	145	2.2	2.5	2.2	4.9	3.3	7.3
73	160	1.3	2.8	2.5	5.5	3.7	8.1
79	175	1.4	3.1	2.6	6.0	4.0	8.9
86	190	1.5	3.4	2.9	6.5	4.3	9.6
102	225	1.8	3.9	3.5	7.7	5.1	11.3
113	250	2.0	4.3	3.9	8.6	5.7	12.7

Given below is another table showing how much energy is spent in different types of physical activities:

Type of the physical activity	Energy spent in an hour
1. Walking	125 to 200 calories
2. Household chores	150 to 250 calories
3. Fast walking	300 to 350 calories
4. Gardening	300 to 350 calories
5. Games like kho-kho and kabaddi	300 to 350 calories
6. Table tennis	325 to 375 calories
7. Light exercises of yoga	350 to 400 calories
8. Cycling	400 to 450 calories
9. Dancing	400 to 500 calories
10. Lawn tennis or Badminton	400 to 500 calories
11. Swimming	550 to 700 calories
12. Skipping	650 to 700 calories
13. Running	650 to 800 calories
14. Heavy exercises	700 to 1000 calories

Note: When energy worth 3500 calories is spent, the weight is reduced by 1 pound.

The exercises, thus, help a person to spend energy and reduce his weight. This is an apparent benefit of the exercise. The exercise yields another less apparent benefit also. It increases the basal metabolic rate of the body which in turn burns away the excess fat. The increase in this rate is proportionate to the intensity of the exercise. Following a session of heavy exercise, this rate is sustained at a very high level for hours together[5]. In the past, people have underestimated the importance of the exercise as they did not take into account this increase in basal metabolic rate.

However, here is a word of caution. It is not advisable to launch heavy exercises suddenly or without any previous experience. It is desirable that the exercises should be increased gradually.

It is now a conclusively established fact that exercises cause no additional burden on the different organs or systems of the body. In fact, they avert dreadful consequences of obesity. Exercises help a person to lower his blood-pressure. They also reduce the level of lipids in the blood and improve the body's sensitivity to the hormone insulin. Exercises make the heart stronger and more efficient. They reduce the possibilities of coronary heart disease.[7]

It has also been noticed that in any slimming programme through dieting alone, 75% of the weight reduction is due to the loss of fat and the remaining 25% is due to loss of cells which are useful to the body. But if the dieting is accompanied by the exercises also, the loss of useful cells is restricted only to 5%.

The exercises improve the muscle tone and remove wrinkles and flabbiness of skin.[8]

As indicated earlier, sometimes, psychological disorders are also associated with obesity. The exercises improve the mental health. It has been noticed that those persons who at one time suffered restlessness or anxiety become tranquil and mentally balanced after starting regular exercises.[9] In one of the experiments, it was also noticed that there was a positive improvement in the self-respect and will-power of some young lads who did exercises regularly[10].

In this way, exercises yield a definite psychological gain, increase fitness and muscle tone and inspire self-confidence. In modern times, the factor of psychological health is accepted as an integral part of the concept of total health. It is an added advantage that improvement in the mental health helps in maintaining the correct weight afterwards also.[11]

The right time for exercises: Researches have proved that the exercises yield better results if they are divided into 2 or 3 sessions at different times during the day. The first session should be scheduled half an hour before the morning breakfast. It causes mild ketosis in the body and commences the consumption of the accumulated fat.[12] Other sessions should begin after about 3 to $3\frac{1}{2}$ hours following the meals. They burn away the extra food before it is transformed into fat.

These are recommended timings for the exercises. However, they can be done profitably at any convenient hour of the day.

Who can do what type of exercises?: (1) Women can treat their household chores as exercises. This can easily be done by reducing dependence on the servants. They can do some yogasanas also.

(2) The exercise of walking or jogging is generally convenient to everyone. Walking long distances early in the

morning and inhaling fresh air makes the body, mind and soul healthy and pure. Deep breathing is essential during long walks.

(3) The exercise of Yogasanas is convenient for everyone.

(4) Children and youngsters can get enough exercise by participating in different games and sports.

(5) The exercise of skipping is very good for girls.

(6) Elderly people and middle-aged can do the exercise by going for long walks or by doing gardening.

(7) Those who are very busy and can't spare any time for the exercise can also increase their energy expenditure either by standing for longer durations during the day or by cutting down their usual hours of sleep. It has been noticed that when fat persons are sleeping or relaxing, their basal metabolic rate is reduced to almost nil.

Some suggestions for exercises:

(1) Do not be overenthusiastic with the exercises. In the beginning, do only light exercises. Their duration and intensity should be gradually increased keeping pace with the improvement in your health, vitality and efficiency of various organs.

(2) In the beginning do not undertake those heavy exercises that could exhaust you, make you breathless or perspire profusely. The very purpose of exercises is defeated if they tire you out so much that you have to take rest for the rest of the day.

(3) Regularity is very essential in the exercise. The efficacy of the exercise depends on the regularity. Do not miss a single day in the exercise programme. Never succumb to your instinct to turn lazy and give up the exercise.

Synopsis:

1. Lack of adequate physical activity is one of the major causes of obesity.
2. Do not fuss over the fact that the exercise will increase your hunger.
3. In some cases, dieting alone fails to remove the excess fat; so it should be accompanied by the exercise. This combination produces the desired result.
4. Everyone of us can undertake the exercise in any convenient form.

References:

1. Silverstone. J. T., Gordon, R. P. & Stunkard, A. J. (1969)–Social factors in obesity in London. *Practitioner*, 202, 682.
2. Bullen, B. A., Read, R. B. & Mayer, J. (1964)–Physical activity of obese and non-obese adolescent girls appraised by motion picture sampling. *Am. J. Clin. Nutr.*, 14, 211.
3. Mayor, J., Roy, P. & Mitra, K. P. (1956)–Relation between caloric intake, body weight and physical work. *Am. J. publ. Hlth.* 60, 679.
4. Bjorntorp, P. (1976)–In *Clinical Endocr.* Metab. 5, 2,431.
5. Edwards, H. T. et al (1935)–The energy requirements in strenuous muscular exercise, *New Engl. J. Med., 213, 532.*
6. *Pollock. M. L., Wilmore, J. H. & Fox, S. M. (1978)–Health and Fitness through Physical Activity,* Wiley, New York.
7. Fox, S. M., Naughton, J. P. & Haskell, W. L. (1971)–Physical activity in prevention of coronary heart disease, *Ann. Clin. Res.*, 3 : 404-432.
8. Bloom, W. L. (1968)–To fast or to exercise, *Am. J. Clin. Nutr.*, 21, 1475.
9. Folkins, C. H. & Sime, W. E. (1981)–Physical fitness training and mental health, *Am. Psychol.*, 36:373-389.
10. Collingwood, T. R. & Willet, L. (1971)–The effects of physical training upon self-concept and body attitudes, *Clin. Psychol.*, 27:411-412.
11. Cohen, E. A. et al (1980)–Self-control practices associated with weight-loss maintenance in children and adolescents, *Behav. Therapy.* 11:26-37.
12. Richard Mackarness (1970)–*Eat fat and grow slim,* Pocket Books, New York.

Note: Exercises suggested in this chapter are meant for men as well as women.

11. MAKE YOUR BODY SHAPELY WITH EXERCISE

Fat generally accumulates on specific parts of the body, such as, chin, neck, belly and waist in case of men, and breasts, back, waist, abdomen, thighs and hips in case of women. Due to the accumulated fat, the body looks ugly and out of shape.

But there is no need to lose heart and surrender to such a situation. It is possible to discard the excess fat and bring your body in shape once again with the help of exercises. Here is a 'four-week programme' for reducing your weight. This programme certainly restores the body its original shape. **The programme is meant for both–men and women.**

Some preparatory actions, which necessarily precede the daily exercises, are called 'Warm-up'.

Why warm-up?

(1) Warm-up actions help in loosening the muscles and removing their stiffness.

(2) They prepare the muscles for the exercise.

(3) They warm-up the muscles. This is necessary because cold muscles are prone to injuries.

(4) They reduce the possibility of post-exercise pain in muscles and joints.

(5) They prepare the lungs and the heart for the exercise.

(6) They reduce the general stiffness of the body.

Warm-up actions:

(1) Spot running: Stand in one place and run for two to three minutes. Keep the pace slow in the beginning and increase it gradually. Every time lift the knee as high as you can.

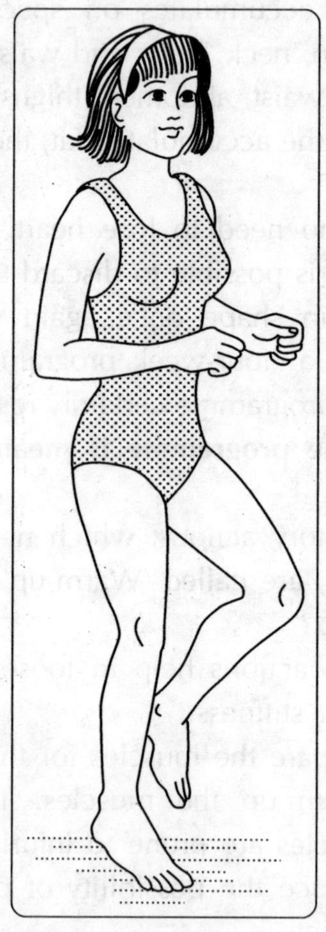

Fig. 16

(2) Shoulder movements: Move your shoulders up and down as shown in the picture. Keep your fists tightly-closed. Inhale while lifting up the shoulders and exhale as you lower your shoulders. Repeat this action for two minutes.

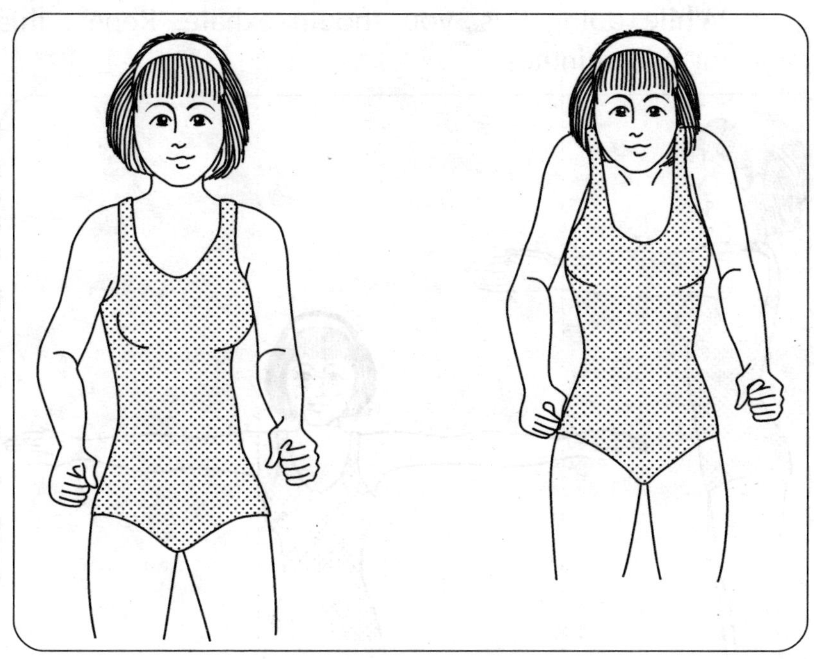

Fig. 17

(3) Expansion of chest: Stand erect as shown in the picture, keeping a little distance between your feet. Extend both your hands straight in line with the shoulders. Then move them on both the sides. While doing this inhale deeply. Bring both the hands in the original position once again. While doing this, you should exhale. Repeat this action for two minutes.

Fig. 18

(4) Parvatasana-Hastpadasana: These two asanas have to be done alternately. Begin with Parvatasana. Inhale deeply while bending the body backwards; and while exhaling, bend your body forwards. Repeat these actions slowly for two minutes.

Fig. 19

Note: These four actions constitute the warm-up. Do them before starting your daily exercise-session.

Some suggestions:

(1) Do the exercises on an empty stomach. Early morning is the ideal time for doing the exercises. However, they can be done after an interval of about 3 to $3\frac{1}{2}$ hours after the lunch.

(2) Empty your urinary bladder before starting the exercises.

(3) The pace of doing exercises varies from person to person. So you may do them at the pace that suits you.

(4) While doing the exercises if you get breathless, it is an indication that you need to reduce your pace.

(5) At the end of the exercises, you should not feel too tired. Do not do the exercises at such a pace that you are exhausted when you are through with them.

(6) When you are through with the warm-up actions and all the exercises, perform Shavasana for five minutes.

Technique for Shavasana: Lie flat. Keep your eyes closed. Relax all the muscles of your body. In this condition, the body should look like a corpse. Slow down your breathing to such an extent that a spectator should feel as if you are not breathing at all. Calm down your mind and keep it linked to the thoughts of God. Give prior instructions to your family members that they should not disturb you while you are doing this. There is no better remedy than Shavasana which relaxes the mind and affords the maximum rest in the minimum time.

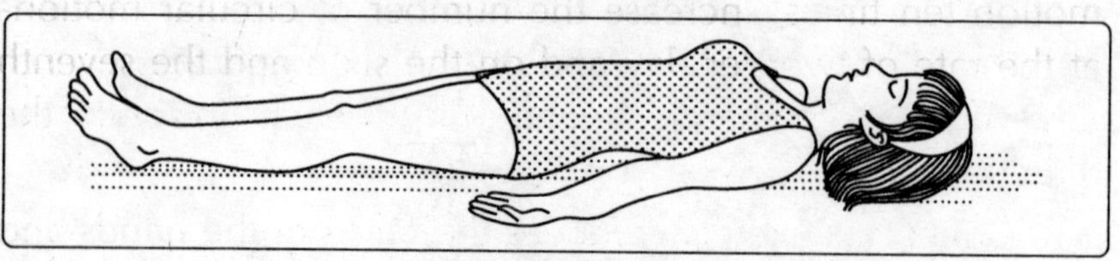

Fig. 20

EXERCISES TO BRING YOUR BODY BACK IN SHAPE

FIRST WEEK

Note: Perform all the four actions of warm-up before commencing the exercises.

EXERCISE 1

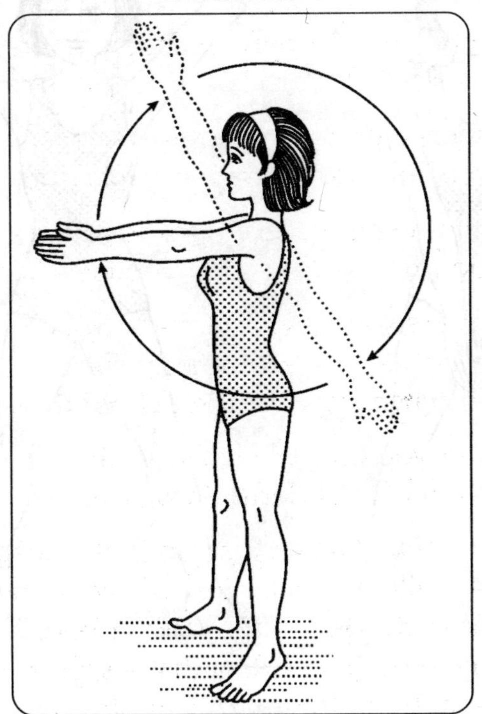

Fig. 21

Stand erect keeping a distance of about $1'$ to $1\frac{1}{2}'$ between your two feet. At first keep both your arms straight and then move them forwards and backwards in circular motion ten times. Increase the number of circular motions at the rate of two per day and on the sixth and the seventh day move your hands twenty times each in both the directions.

Gain: This exercise reduces the fat from the hands and the shoulders and also lends them good shape.

EXERCISE 2

Fig. 22

Stand erect keeping a distance of about 1′ to $1\frac{1}{2}$′ between your two feet. Keep both your arms in front of your thighs, as shown in the picture. Now inhale and raise both the arms to an oblique position. Now exhale and bring your hands down to the original position. Repeat this action ten times. The frequency of the action should be raised at the rate of one per day so that on the seventh day the action is repeated sixteen times.

Gain: This exercise reduces the fat from the chest and makes the breasts firm and shapely.

EXERCISE 3

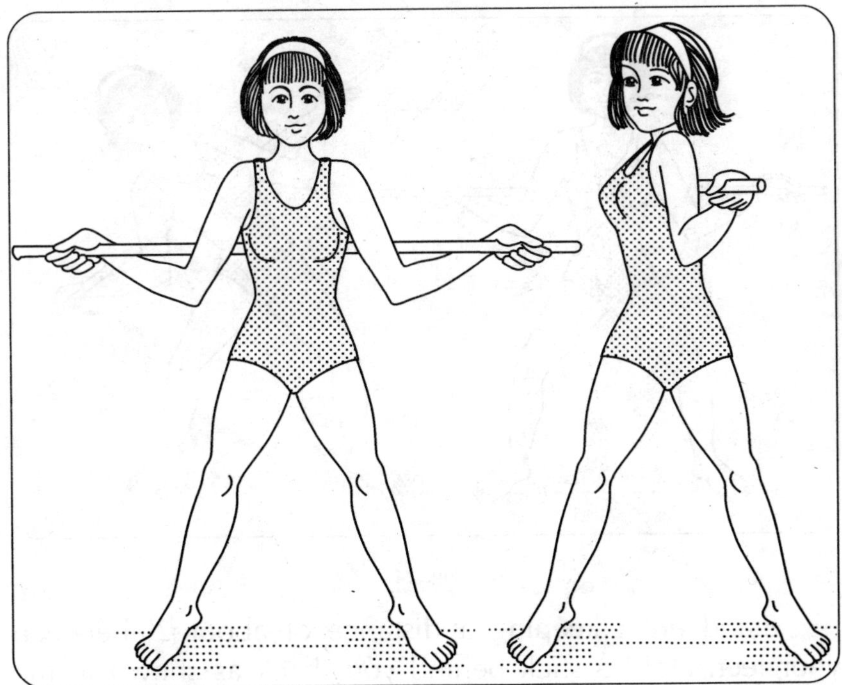

Fig. 23

Stand erect keeping a distance of about 1′ to $1\frac{1}{2}$′ between your feet. Hold a stick behind your back, as shown in the picture. Now twist the upper portion of your body to left as much as you can. Remember your legs and thighs should remain straight. Now revert back to the original position. Now twist the body to the right as much as you can. Again revert to the original position. Twist the body ten times in each direction.

Gain: This exercise reduces the fat from the waist and makes it slim and shapely.

EXERCISE 4

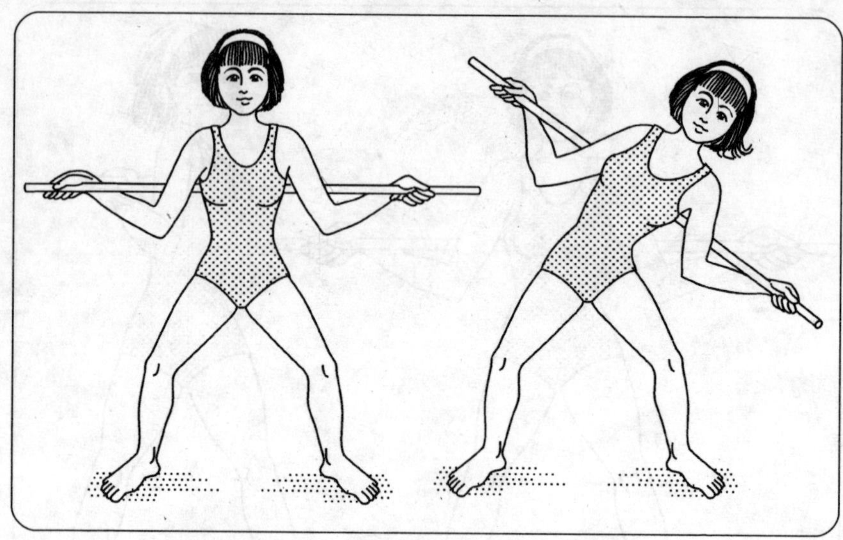

Fig. 24

Stand erect keeping a distance of about 2′ between your feet. Hold a stick behind your back as shown in the picture. Now tilt your body to the left. While doing so, the body should not move; it should only be tilted on one side. Revert back to the original position. Now tilt your body to the right without moving it. Revert back to the original position. Tilt the body ten times in each direction.

Gain : This exercise reduces the fat from the waist and makes it slim and shapely.

EXERCISE 5

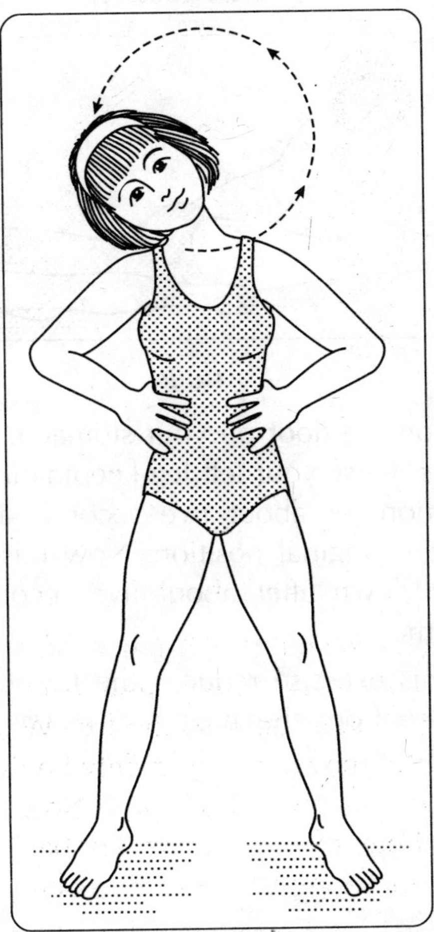

Fig. 25

Stand erect keeping a distance of about 1′ to $1\frac{1}{2}'$ between your feet. Now keep your body steady and move your head five times in the clockwise circular motion. Then move it five times in the anti-clockwise direction. In all, move your head twenty times. Every time try to tilt your head as much as you can. Do this exercise slowly or else it might cause giddiness.

Gain: This exercise reduces the fat from the neck.

EXERCISE 6

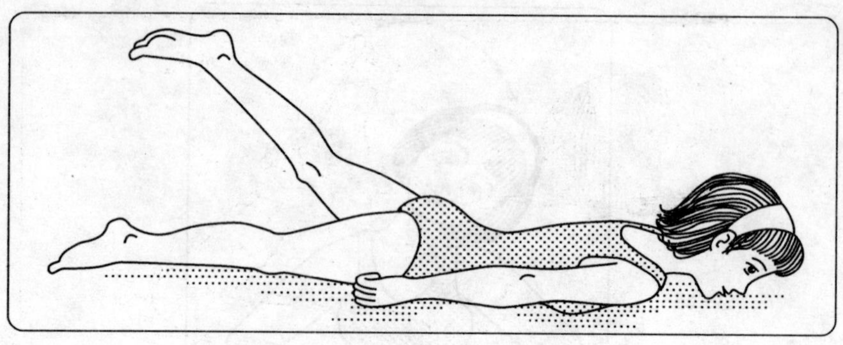

Fig. 26

Lie flat on the floor on your stomach. Keep your arms by your sides. Raise your left leg keeping it straight. Keep it in that position for about five seconds and then slowly lower it to the original position. Now raise your right leg and bring it down after about five seconds. Repeat this action ten times.

Gain: This exercise reduces the fat not only from the waist but also from the hips and makes them firm and shapely.

EXERCISE 7

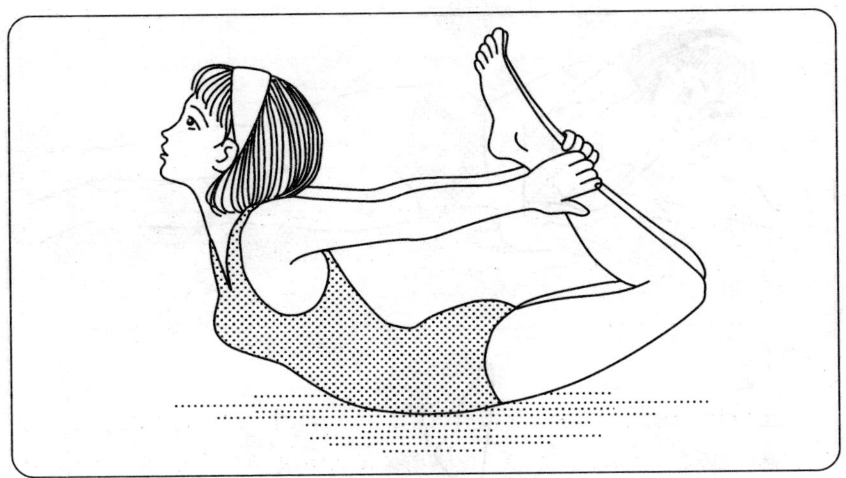

Fig. 27

Lie on the floor facing downward. Bend the legs inward at the knees. Raise the arms and grip the ankles firmly. Raise your chest and head. Your posture will form a beautiful arch. Now, like a pendulum, rock your body slowly forwards and backwards. After rocking your body twenty times in both the directions, leave your legs and revert to the original position.

Gain: This exercise reduces the fat from the stomach and the back and makes the stomach firm.

EXERCISE 8

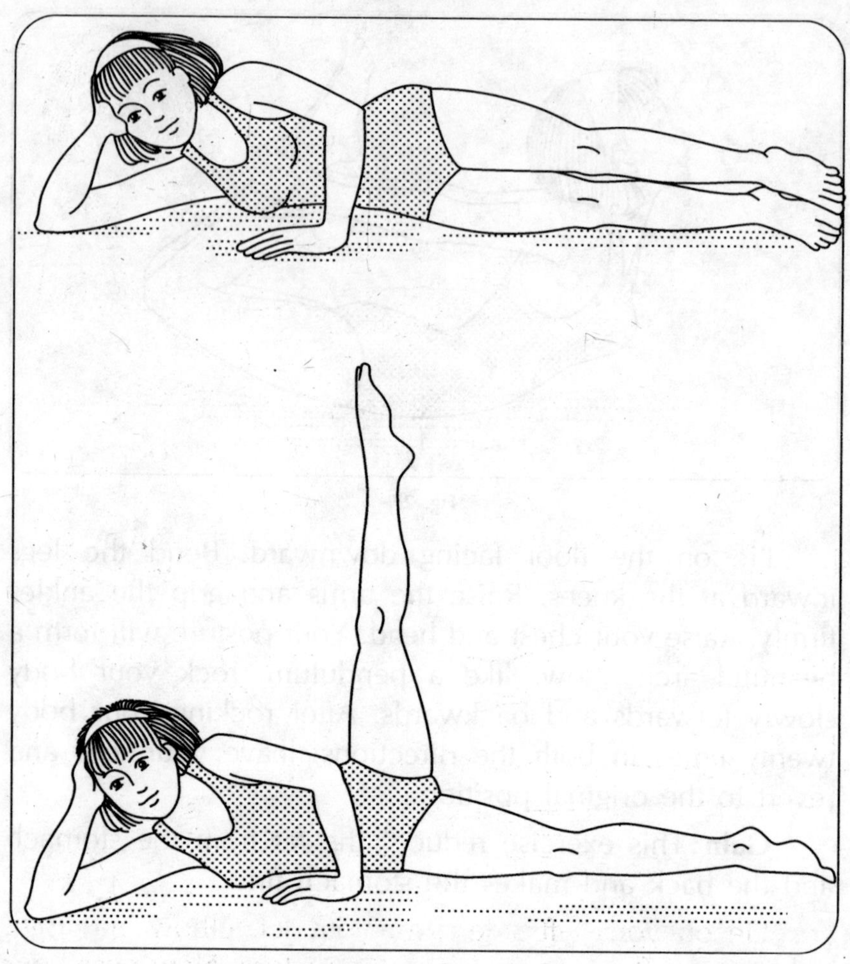

Fig. 28

Lie on your right side. Rest your head on your right palm and rest the right elbow on the floor. Now extend your leg as high as you can. Then slowly bring it back to the original position. Repeat this action ten times. Then lie on your left side and extend your right leg upward ten times.

Gain: This exercise reduces the fat from the thighs and the waist and makes the outer muscles of your thighs firm.

EXERCISE 9

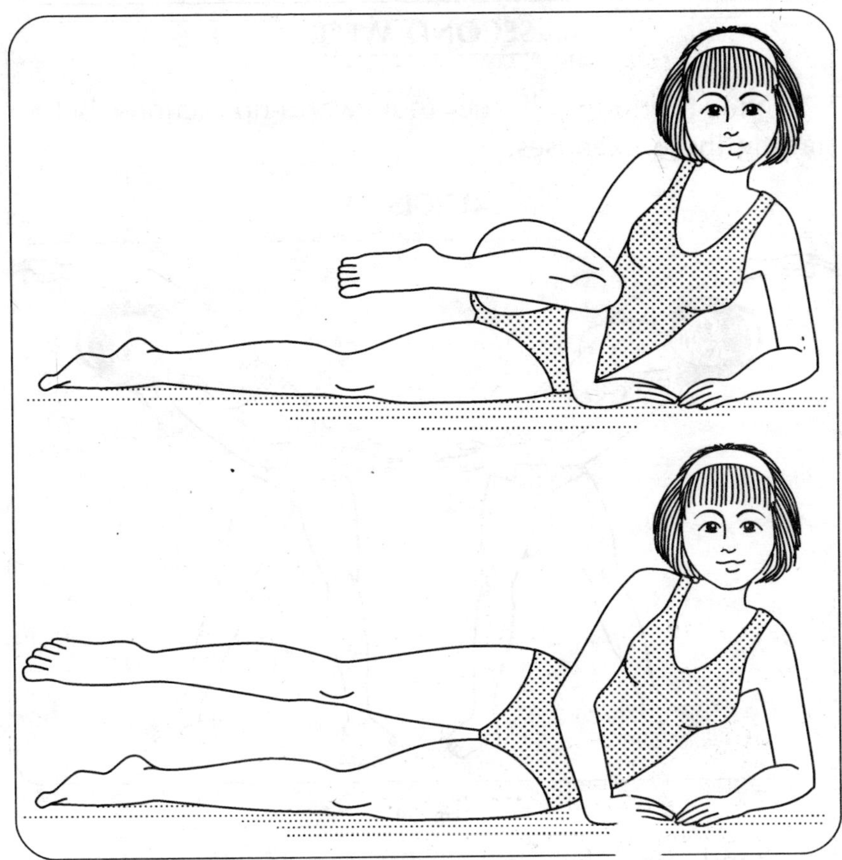

Fig. 29

Lie on your left side. Rest your left elbow and right palm on the floor, as shown in the picture. Now raise your right leg slightly and kick in the air. Repeat this action ten times. Now lie on your right side and kick ten times with your left leg.

Gain: This exercise reduces the fat from the thighs and makes them shapely.

Note: During the first week, all these nine exercises have to be performed everyday. Don't forget to perform 'Shavasana' after all the exercises are over.

EXERCISES TO BRING YOUR BODY BACK IN SHAPE

SECOND WEEK

Note : Perform all the four warm-up actions before starting these exercises.

EXERCISE 1

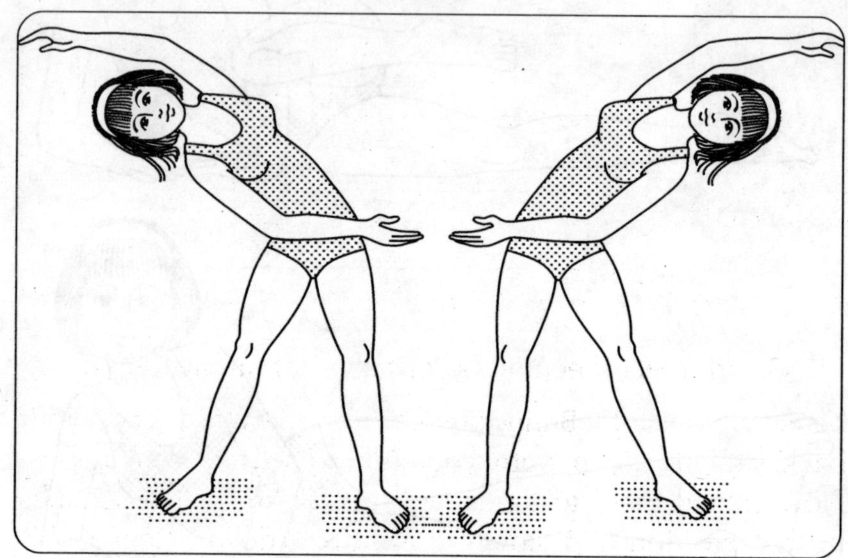

Fig. 30

Stand erect keeping a distance of about 1′ to $1\frac{1}{2}'$ between your two feet. Keep both your arms hanging along your sides in line with the shoulders. Now extend your right arm downward and left arm upward as shown in the picture, and tilt your body to the right. Soon afterwards do this action in the reverse order, i.e., tilt your body to the left and extend your right arm upward and left arm downward. Repeat both the actions ten times each.

Gain : This exercise reduces the fat from the waist and makes it slim and shapely.

EXERCISE 2

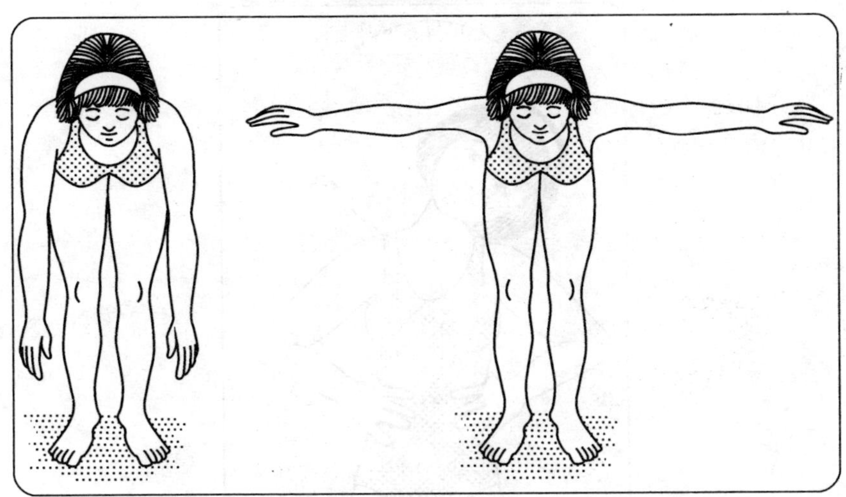

Fig. 31

Stand erect keeping a distance of about 1′ to $1\frac{1}{2}$′ between your feet. Bend forward from the waist. Keep your back straight. Keep both your arms hanging from above. Now extend them to the sides, keep them for ten seconds in that position and slowly bring them down. Repeat this action ten times.

Gain : This exercise reduces the fat from the shoulders and the back.

EXERCISE 3

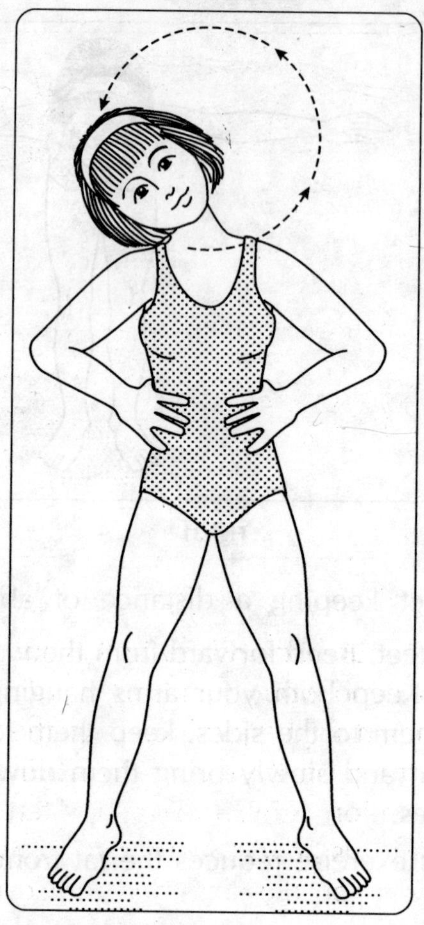

Fig. 32

Stand erect keeping a distance of about 1′ to $1\frac{1}{2}'$ between your two feet. Now keep the body steady and rotate your head. Rotate it five times in the clockwise direction and five times in the anticlockwise direction. In all, move your head thirty times. While rotating your head, every time try to tilt it as much as you can. Perform these actions slowly, otherwise it might cause giddiness.

Gain : This exercise reduces the fat from around the neck.

EXERCISE 4

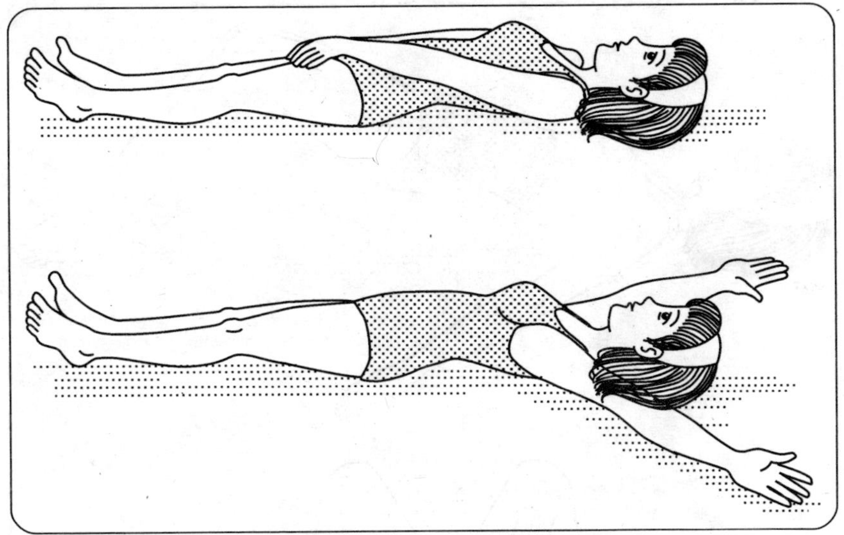

Fig. 33

Lie flat on your back. Place both your hands on your thighs. Then extend your hands upwards in an oblique direction as shown in the picture. Take them beyond your head and rest them on the floor. Now bring them back to their original position. Repeat this action ten times. Increase the frequency of this action at the rate of two per day and do it twenty times on the sixth and the seventh day.

Gain: This exercise reduces the fat from the chest and makes the breasts firm and proportionate.

EXERCISE 5

Fig. 34

Lie flat on your back. Now bend your legs from the knees as shown in the picture and lift your body. The weight of your entire body should rest on your legs and shoulders. Now lower your hips slowly. Repeat this action ten times.

Gain : This exercise reduces the fat from the hips and makes them firm.

EXERCISE 6

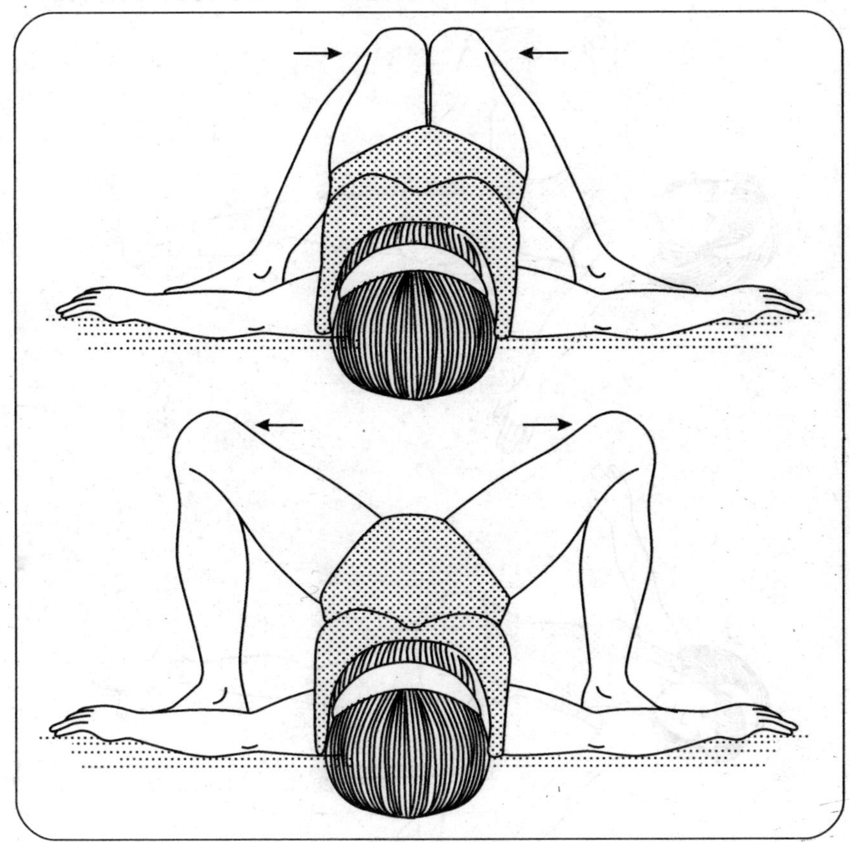

Fig. 35

Lie flat on your back. Bend your legs from the knees. Keep a distance of about 1′ to $1\frac{1}{2}$′ between your two feet. Like the previous exercise, lift your body in such a way that the weight of the body rests on your feet and shoulders. Then keep your feet steady and move your thighs outwards in the opposite directions. Now bring them back together. Repeat this action ten times.

Gain: This exercise reduces the fat from the thighs and the hips and makes them shapely.

EXERCISE 7

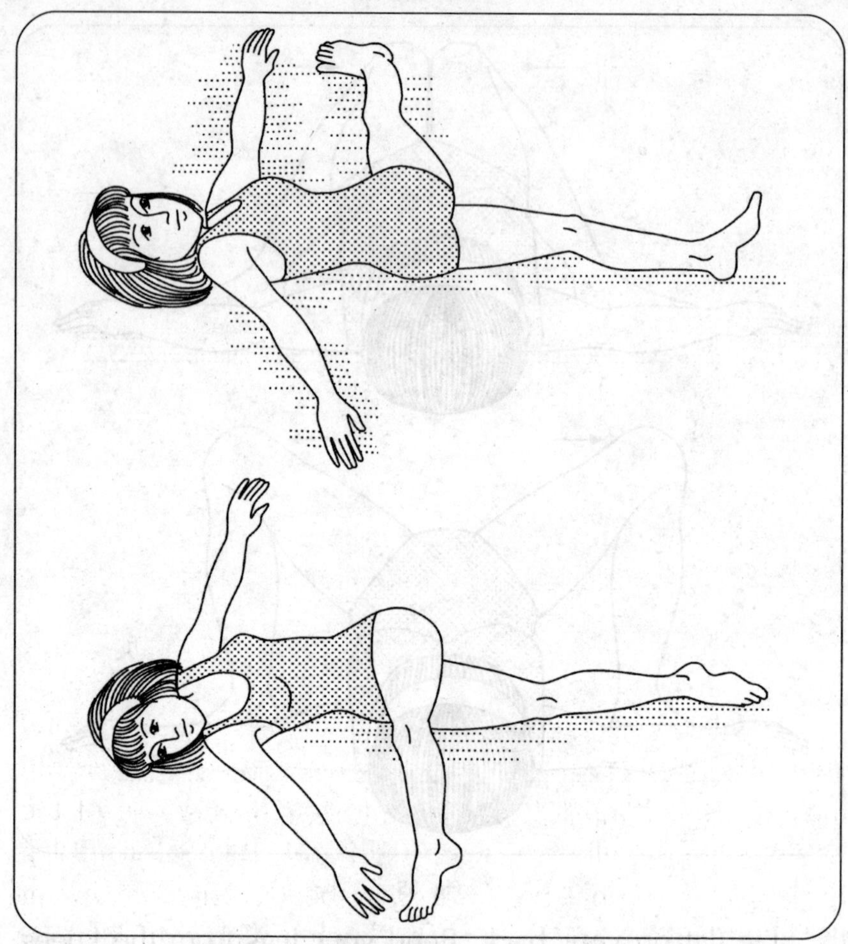

Fig. 36

Lie flat on your back. Keep both your arms spread at the sides. Your palms should touch the floor. Now raise your left leg and bring it down in such a way that it touches the fingers of your right hand. Now revert to your original position. Then perform the same type of action with your right leg. Repeat this action ten times with each leg.

Gain: This exercise reduces the fat from the thighs and the abdomen and makes them firm and shapely.

EXERCISE 8

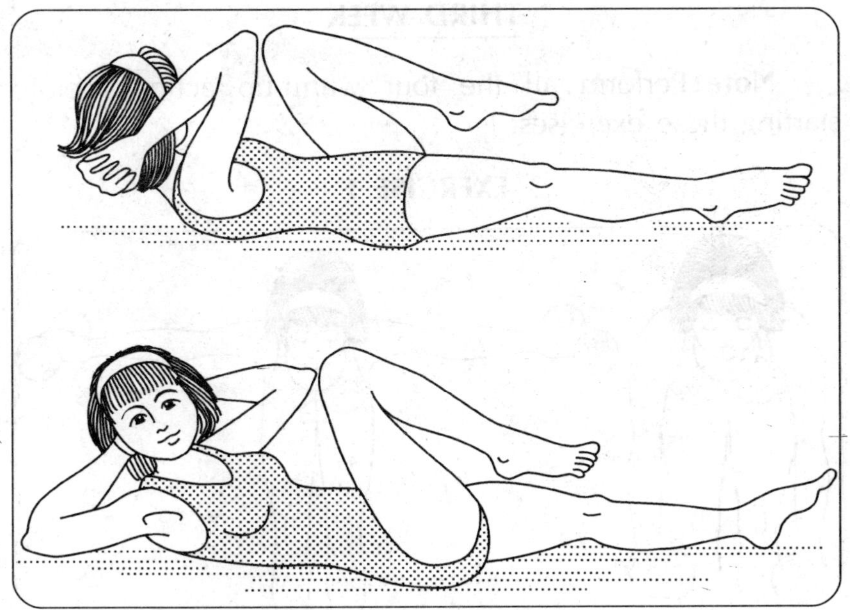

Fig. 37

Lie flat on your back. Clasp both your palms behind your head. Now bend your left leg at the knee as shown in the picture and raise it. Now try to touch the knee of the left leg with the elbow of your right arm. Take your left leg back to the original position. Now bend your right leg at the knee, raise it and then try to touch it with your left-arm elbow. Repeat each action ten times.

Gain: This exercise helps in reducing the fat from the abdomen and the waist.

Note: During the second week, these 8 exercises have to be performed everyday. Perform Shavasana after the exercises.

EXERCISES TO BRING YOUR BODY BACK IN SHAPE

THIRD WEEK

Note : Perform all the four warm-up actions before starting these exercises.

EXERCISE 1

Fig. 38

Stand erect keeping a little distance between your feet. Now bend forward from your waist. The back should remain straight. Now hold a pair of dumbells, one each, in your hands. Keep both your arms hanging downward. Now lift your arms and take them in opposite directions. After 10 counts, bring them down slowly. Repeat this action ten times.

Gain : This exercise reduces the excess fat from your arms, shoulders and the back and makes them shapely.

EXERCISE 2

Fig. 39

Stand erect keeping a distance of about 2′ to $2\frac{1}{2}'$ between your feet. Keep both your arms straight in line with your shoulders. Now extend your left arm downwards and try to touch your left foot with your left hand. At the same time take your right arm straight upwards. Now revert back to the original position. Then try to touch your right foot with your right hand and take your left arm straight upward. Now revert once again to your original position. Repeat each action ten times.

Gain : This exercise reduces unwanted fat from the waist and makes it shapely.

EXERCISE 3

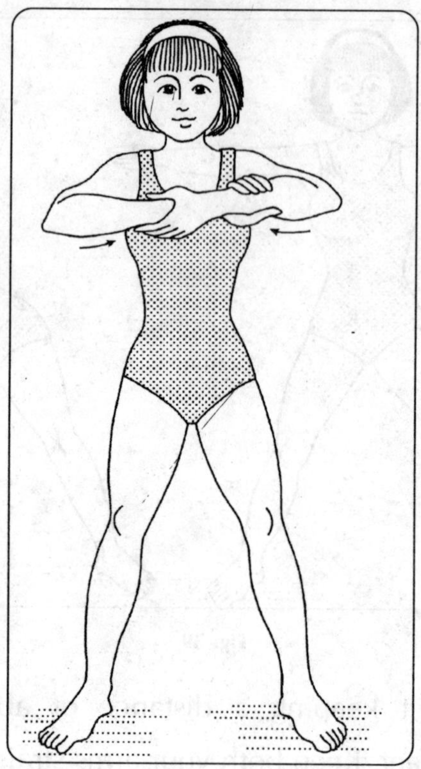

Fig. 40

Stand erect keeping a distance of about $1\frac{1}{2}'$ to $2'$ between your two feet. Now hold each of your arms near the elbow with the other palm as shown in the picture. Keep your arms in front of your chest about four inches away from your body. Now try to apply pressure on your left elbow with your right hand to push it in the outer direction. Similarly, try to push your right elbow with your left hand. Release the pressure after about five seconds. Repeat this action twenty times.

Gain : This exercise reduces the excess fat from the chest, and makes the chest and the breasts firm and shapely.

EXERCISE 4

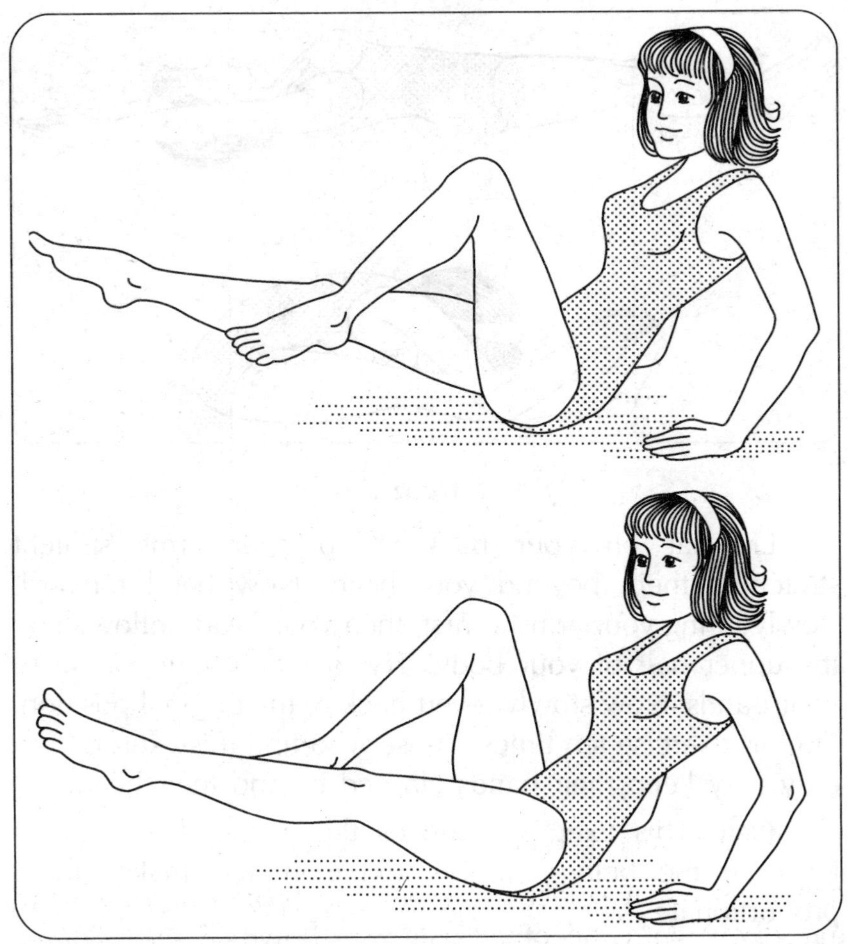

Fig. 41

Squat on the floor. Keep your legs straight. Place your palms on the floor behind your body. As shown in the picture, tilt your body in such a way that its weight is distributed on both the arms. Now raise your legs slightly up and move them as if you are cycling. Continue to do this action as long as you can.

Gain: This exercise reduces the excess fat from the thighs and the abdomen and makes them proportionate.

EXERCISE 5

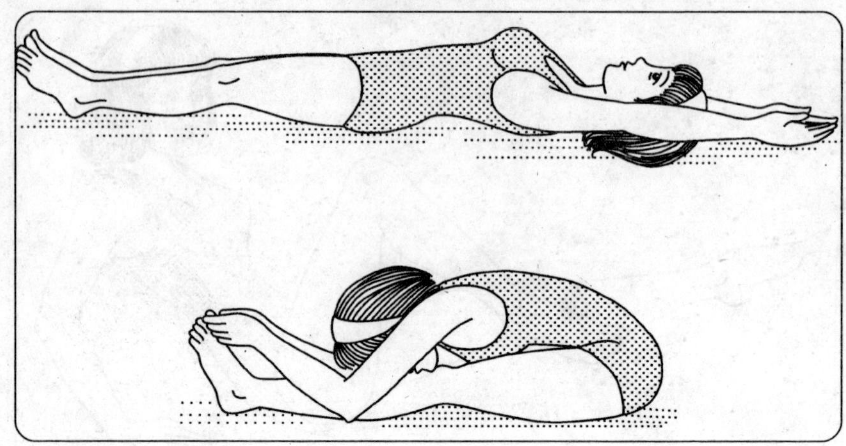

Fig. 42

Lie flat on your back. Keep your arms straight stretching them beyond your head. Now bend forward, slowly lifting your arms at first, then your head, followed by the upper half of your body. Try to touch your toes with your hands. Now slowly revert back to the original position. Do this exercise ten times. Those who find this exercise too easy may keep their hands clasped behind their head.

Gain: This exercise reduces the accumulated excess fat from the belly and the abdomen and makes them proportionate.

EXERCISE 6

Fig. 43

Lie on your stomach facing downward. Keep your arms straight by your sides. Now keep your legs straight and lift them slowly from the floor. After about five seconds, lower them slowly. Repeat this action ten times.

Those who find this exercise very easy should keep their arms stretched straight above their head, and along with their legs, they should lift their arms and the upper half of the body also.

Gain: This exercise reduces the fat from the waist and the buttocks and makes them shapely.

EXERCISE 7

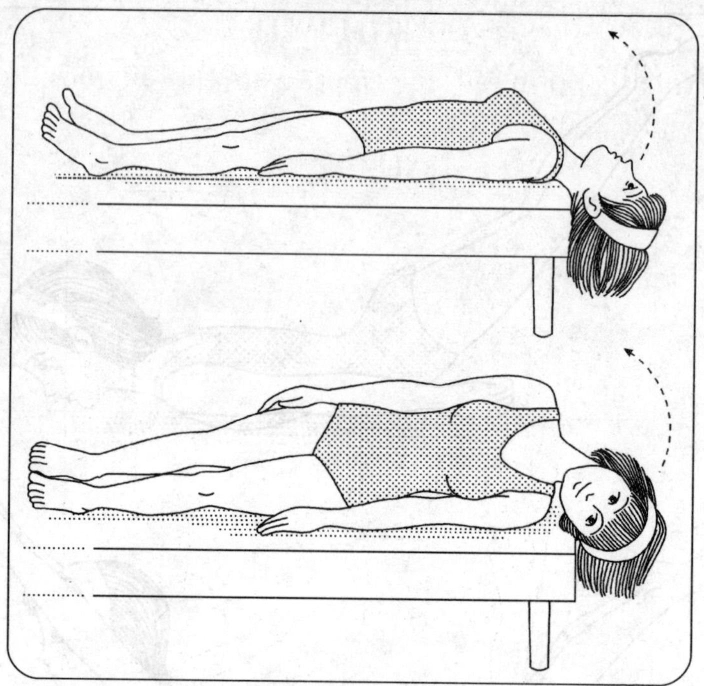

Fig. 44

Lie flat on a bench or a settee in such a way that your head can hang freely from above. Allow the head to remain tilted downward. Now lift your head slowly. After about five seconds, allow the head to drop back slowly to its original position. Repeat this action 10 times.

Now turn and lie on your left side. Keep your head hanging as before. Slowly lift your head up. After about five seconds, lower it slowly. Repeat this action ten times.

Now turn and lie on the right side and perform this action ten times.

Gain: This exercise reduces the unwanted fat from and around the neck and makes it shapely.

> **Note:** During the third week, all these seven exercises have to be performed everyday. Perform Shavasana after all the seven exercises are over.

EXERCISES TO BRING YOUR BODY BACK IN SHAPE

FOURTH WEEK

Note: Perform all the four warm-up actions before starting these exercises.

EXERCISE 1

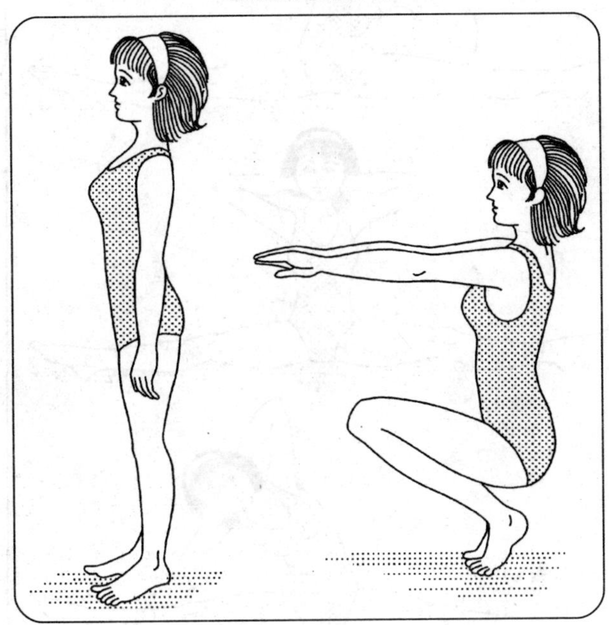

Fig. 45

Stand erect keeping a distance of about six inches between your feet. Keep the toes slightly apart in an oblique position. Now bend your knees and lower the body slowly. Along with this, slowly raise your heels so that the weight of the body is transferred on to the toes. Simultaneously raise both your arms in such a way that they are in line with the shoulders. Now revert back slowly to the original standing position. Perform this action ten times. Increase the frequency of this exercise at the rate of two per day, and do it twenty times on the sixth and the seventh day.

Gain: This exercise reduces the excess fat from the thighs very soon and makes them firm and shapely.

EXERCISE 2

Fig. 46

Squat on the floor. Keep your legs wide apart in opposite directions as much as you can. Clasp your hands and keep them behind your head in such a way that the palms touch the back of your head. Now tilt your body and try to touch the right knee with your right hand elbow. Revert back to the original position and tilt your body to the left in order to touch the left knee with your left hand elbow. Tilt your body ten times each to the right and to the left.

Gain: This exercise reduces fat from the waist and makes it slim and shapely.

EXERCISE 3

Fig. 47

Lie flat on your back. Now bend your legs at the knees as shown in the picture and lift your body up. Transfer the weight of your body on both your feet and shoulders. Now lower your hips slowly and then raise them again. Repeat this action twenty times.

Gain : This exercise reduces unwanted fat from the hips and makes them proportionate and shapely.

EXERCISE 4

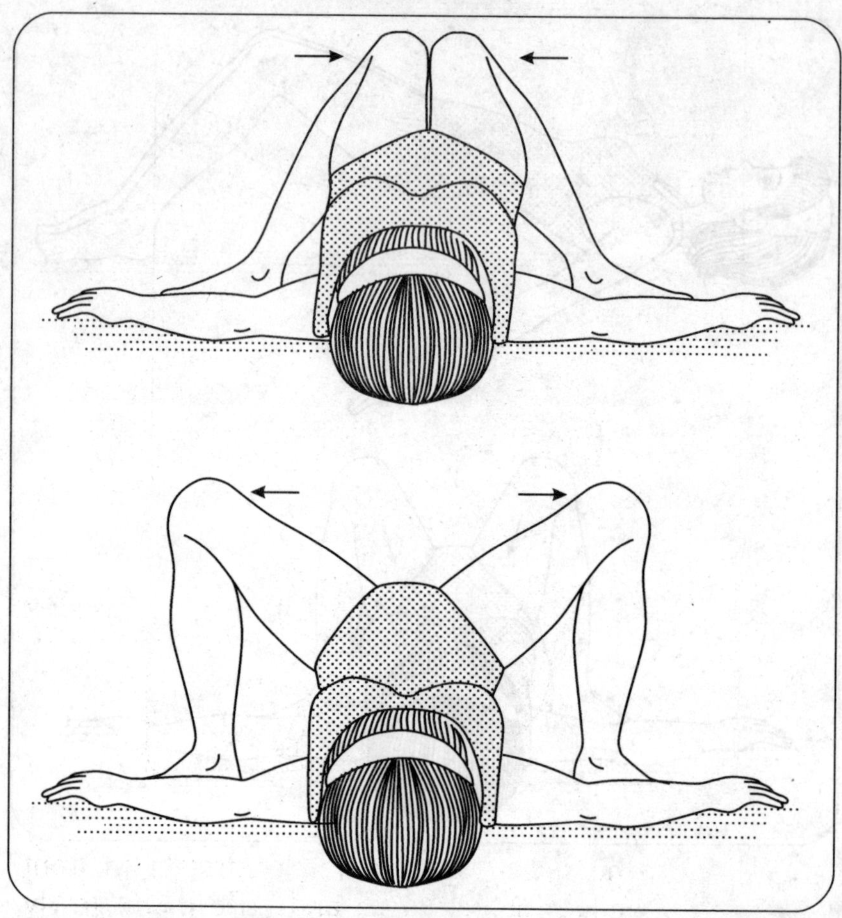

Fig. 48

Lie flat on your back. Bend your legs at the knees. Keep a distance of about $1\frac{1}{2}'$ to $2'$ between your feet. Raise your body in such a way that its weight is transferred on both your feet and shoulders. Now keep your feet steady and move your thighs to the outer direction. Then move them inward once again. Repeat this action twenty times.

Gain: This exercise reduces fat from the thighs and the hips and makes them firm and shapely.

EXERCISE 5

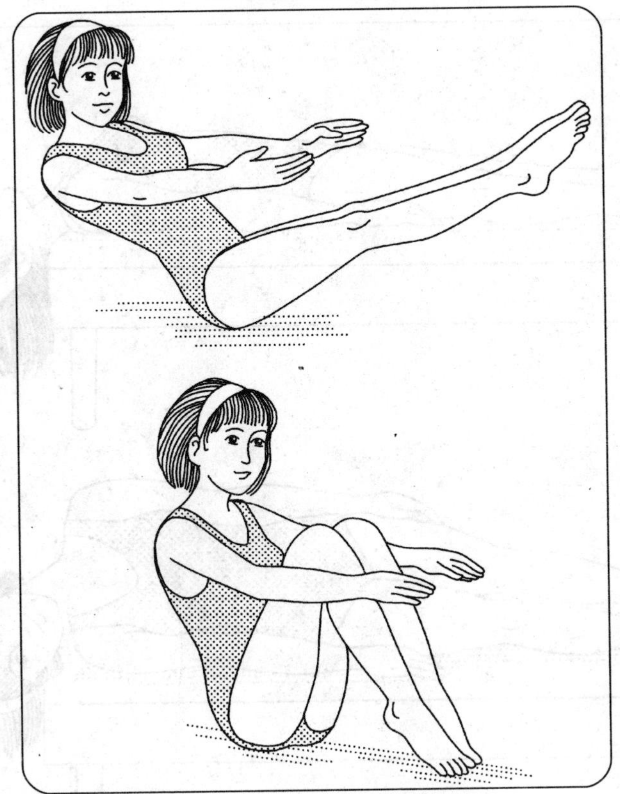

Fig. 49

Squat on the floor. Keep your legs straight in front. Now bend your legs at the knees and raise them slowly. Keep your arms straight ahead in line with the shoulders. The entire weight of the body will rest on your buttocks. This is the initial posture of the exercise. Now slowly straighten your legs and raise them simultaneously. Slowly tilt your body backwards. Then revert back to the initial posture i.e., move the body forwards and bend your legs at the knees and bring your thighs near your body. Perform this action ten times. This is a bit difficult exercise.

Gain: This exercise reduces fat from the belly, the abdomen and the thighs, and makes them shapely.

EXERCISE 6

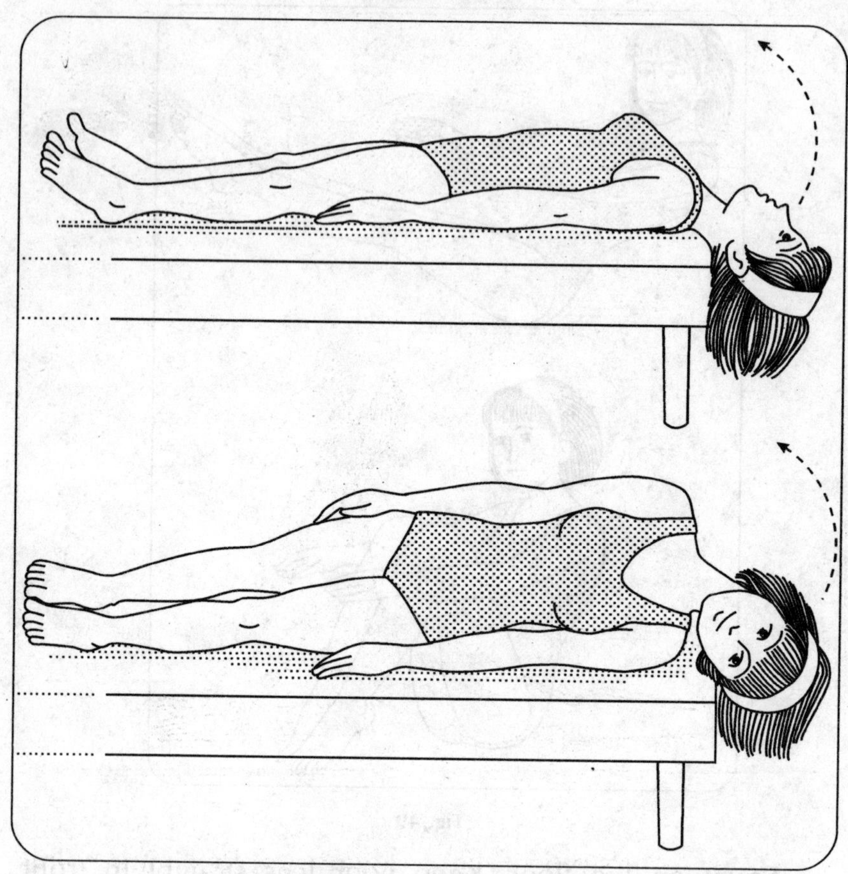

Fig. 50

Description of this action is given on page no. 114 (3rd week – Exercise 7). During the fourth week perform this action twenty times everyday.

Gain : This exercise reduces the unwanted fat from and around the neck and makes it shapely.

EXERCISE 7

Fig. 51

Lie on your stomach, face downward. Rest your palms on the floor in such a way that they are in line with the shoulders. Now first raise your head and then slowly raise the upper half of your body. Form an arch with your spinal cord. See to it that the weight of the body is transferred to the palms as less as possible. After about five seconds, bring the body back to its original position. Perform this action ten times.

Gain: This exercise reduces fat from the back and the arms and makes them shapely.

EXERCISE 8

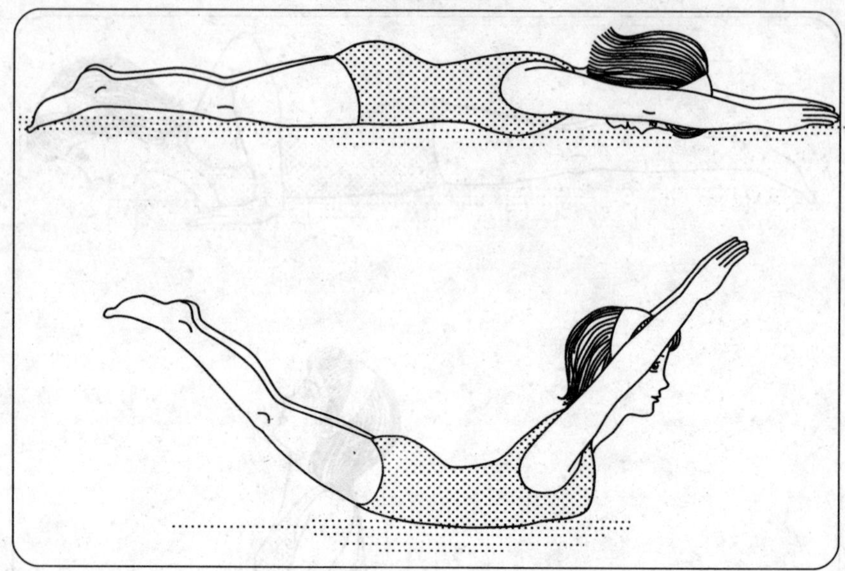

Fig. 52

Lie on your stomach, face downward. Keep your arms extended beyond your head. Now slowly raise your arms, upper half of the body and legs. Form an arch-like posture. After about five seconds, revert back slowly to the original position. Perform this action ten times.

Gain: This exercise reduces the fat from the buttocks, the waist, the hips and the back and makes them shapely.

EXERCISE 9

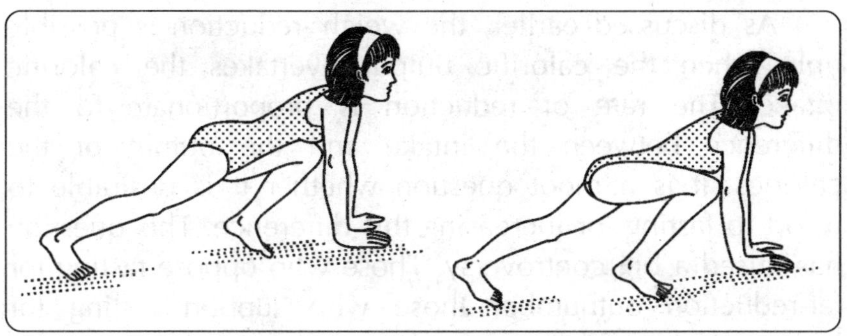

Fig. 53

Make a pose as shown in the picture. Keep both your arms straight downward in line with the shoulders. Keep your right leg straight and bend the left leg at the knee and keep it under your chest. Now bend your right leg at the knee and bring it under your chest. Simultaneously straighten your left leg and take it back. Both the actions should be fast and simultaneous. Perform this action rhythmically for about a minute. Increase the time gradually during the whole week.

Gain : This exercise has a beautiful effect on the entire body in general and the thighs and the legs in particular.

Instruction : These nine exercises have to be performed everyday during the fourth week. Don't miss to perform Shavasana after all the exercises are over.

Note : This four-week programme reduces fat from specific parts of the body. These exercises lend a good shape to the ugly parts of the body. They make flabby and weak muscles firm and strong and tone up the lax skin. **Those who wish to maintain their body in shape should continue the fourth week programme and gradually increase the frequency of each exercise as the practice increases.**

12. FASTING TO REDUCE WEIGHT

As discussed earlier, the weight-reduction is possible only when the calorific output overtakes the calorific intake. The rate of reduction is proportionate to the difference between the intake and the output of the calories. It is a moot question whether it is desirable to resort to fasting for increasing this difference. This question has raised a big controversy. Those who oppose fasting for fat-reduction outnumber those who support fasting for losing weight, and therefore, it is necessary to examine in detail, the arguments presented by the rival camps.

Experiments in fasting for slimming have been done on both the bases, short-term as well as long-term. In U.S.A., Dr. Bloom[1] and in U.K., Dr. Thomson[2] and his colleagues made their patients fast for 7 to 10 days. In 1965, Dr. Benoit[3] made his 70 patients fast for 10 days. At the end of this experiments, it was observed that of the total weight lost, only 35 % of the weight-loss was due to the destruction of fat-cells in the body. For the remaining 65 % of the weight-loss, destruction of other useful cells and organs was responsible. Dr. Ball[4] says that when a person subsists on 800 calorie food, only fat-cells are destroyed. In some cases, it was observed that those who consumed 800 calorie food lost more weight than those who undertook fasting.

Here it would be interesting to quote an anecdote from the life of Napoleon Bonaparte. Napoleon attacked Russia and suffered a defeat at Moscow. His soldiers were really harassed by the severe Russian winter, wild wolves and lack of food. When these soldiers, who were mentally depressed and physically weak, returned to their homeland, doctors who examined them were surprised to note that the reduction in weight was not much in cases of those who had had no food at all. But those soldiers who had made efforts to find out some food and had eaten it, had lost a lot of weight. The doctors, therefore, reached a conclusion that the reduction in weight is more if a person continues to eat some amount of food than fasting altogether. It is likely that the increase in the basal metabolic rate of those who eat something is responsible for such a phenomenon.

However, prolonged fasting certainly increases the percentage of destruction of fat-cells in the body. Dr. Runcie and Dr. Hilditch[5] say that in prolonged fasting a stage comes when 96% of the needs of the body are met with from the accumulated fat in the body. However, it is advisable to undertake any prolonged fasting programme at a hospital only. During this period of prolonged fasting, it is essential to carry out investigations, from time to time, to ascertain the level of uric acid in the blood, urea, electrolytes, hydrogen ions concentration (pH), etc. It is also necessary to carry out tests to ascertain the total and differential count of cells in the blood, functioning of liver and heart, etc. also. During the period of fasting, the blood pressure goes down and ketosis and hyperurecaemia occur. And therefore, during the period of fasting it is essential to measure the blood pressure at regular intervals and examine the urine to ascertain the presence of ketones in it.

Dr. Blondheim[6], Dr. Kaufman and Dr. Bortz[7] claim that in the long run total fasting and subsisting on 800 calorie food yield almost similar results.

During the period of fasting, if appropriate steps are not taken, vitamins and minerals stored in the body begin to deplete. This is not a desirable development.

It is apparently clear that fasting has to be wound up at some stage. And it is a matter of common experience that once a person starts consuming food, his weight begins to increase once again and all his labour and sacrifice are wasted.

It is advisable that those patients who wish to reduce their fat should cultivate proper eating and living habits rather than resort to fasting. Fasting does not serve the purpose. In that case, those who are against fasting argue, and rightly so, that why not reduce the weight by resorting to a low-calorie balanced diet that would cultivate proper eating habits?

Some people, who oppose fasting, argue that fasting is one form of starvation and it may cause a person's death. But this argument is sheer nonsense. In a fat person's body, there is always an adequate storage of nutrition that can fulfil the needs of the body for a long time. Some rare cases of deaths during fasting have been recorded. But it cannot be accepted conclusively that it was fasting that was responsible for causing those deaths. It is more likely that some grave diseases like diabetes, heart disease or cancer which are associated with obesity, were perhaps responsible for causing death in those cases.

It is true that ketosis occurs during fasting. But mild ketosis is never harmful. On the contrary; it is beneficial. Due to ketosis, accumulated fat in the body gets dislodged and is burnt away. Addressing the eleventh annual New England post-graduate assembly at Boston, Massachusettes in 1952. Dr. Edward Pennington had said that the reduction in fat is difficult unless ketosis occurs in the body. In absence of ketosis, formation of new fat may stop but the old accumulated fat would not be destroyed.

There is a grain of truth in argument of the supporters of fasting that to eat a little is more difficult than not to eat at all. In many a case, after fasting for two or three days the appetite begins to wane and does not bother the patient. But eating a little generates further appetite which bothers the patient continuously.

In conclusion we can say that, under normal circumstances, fasting is not advisable for reducing fat. However, for getting rid of stubborn obesity which does not yield to other remedial measures, long-term fasting can be undertaken (if possible, at a hospital) under proper medical supervision. During the period of fasting, it is necessary to ensure adequate intake of water. If lemon drops or fruit-juice are added to the water, the chances of problems created by fasting are reduced almost to nil.

Synopsis:

1. Short-term fasting has been noticed to be useless for reducing the weight.
2. Long-term fasting may be undertaken for curing the stubborn obesity not yielding to other measures. But such an experiment should be undertaken at a hospital under proper medical supervision only.
3. Bad habits of eating and living are generally responsible for obesity. Fasting does not eliminate them.

References:

1. Bloom, W. L. (1959)–Fasting as an introduction to the treatment of obesity. *Metabolism,* 8, 214.
2. Thomson, T. J., Runcie, J. & Miller, V. (1966)–Treatment of obesity by total fasting for up to 249 days. *Lancet,* ii, 992.
3. Benoit, R. L., Martin, R. L. & Walton, R. H. (1965)–Change in body composition during weight reduction in obesity. *Ann. intern. Med.,* 63, 604.
4. Ball M. F. et al (1967)–Comparative effects of caloric restriction and metabolic acceleration on body composition in obesity *Ann. intern. Med.,* 67, 60.
5. Runcie, J. & Hilditch, T. E. (1974)–Energy provision, tissue metabolism and weight-loss in prolonged starvation. *Br. med. J.,* ii, 352.
6. Blondheim, S. H. & Kaufman, N. A. (1965)–Comparison of fasting and 800 to 1000 calorie diets in treatment of obesity. *Lancet,* i, 250.
7. Bortz, W. M. (1969)–A 500 pound weight-loss. *Am. J. Med.* 47,325.

13. DRUGS IN THE TREATMENT OF OBESITY

The question whether it is fair to use drugs for losing the excess fat has generated a great controversy.

In western countries, slimming-pills worth crores of rupees are sold every year. The use of such drugs is increasing in our country also and therefore it is necessary to discuss their advantages and disadvantages.

For reducing the fat, the following five types of drugs are generally administered:

(1) Anti-appetite (anorectic) drugs (Phenylethylamine group of drugs) : This group includes amphetamine, diethylpropion, phentermine, fenfluramine and mazindol, etc.

It is not yet clear how these drugs work. According to one school of thought, these drugs affect the metabolic process of sugar and fat. According to another school of thought, these drugs have a direct effect on the satiety centre located in the brain, as a result of which, loss of appetite occurs.

These drugs yield some positive results in the beginning, but afterwards they give rise to some dangerous side-effects. In Canada and some other countries the use of amphetamine, as a weight reducing agent has been banned. These drugs have the following side-effects:

(a) The central nervous system is unduly stimulated.

(b) Sympathetic nervous system is unnecessarily stimulated and symptoms like dryness of the mouth, blurring of vision, dizziness, palpitations and elevation of the blood pressure occur.

(c) In some cases, complaints of coliky pain and severe contraction of muscles of kidneys were reported.[1]

(d) Sometimes, they cause irritation of the gastro-intestinal tract and consequently complaints of nausea, vomitting and constipation occur.

(e) These drugs are habit forming also. This is a very serious problem. Many cases are recorded in which patients could not give up taking these drugs even after they had served their purpose and were no longer necessary[2]. In this way, sometimes the remedy proves more dangerous than the disease itself.

(f) Some cases of Fenfluramine poisoning are also reported and therefore people are always advised to keep these drugs out of children's reach.

(2) Drugs reducing the level of sugar in blood (e.g. phenformin, metformin) : These drugs cause acidosis and problems in the blood-circulation system and are therefore not safe. They have been banned in the U.S.A. since 1977.

(3) Metabolism stimulators (the thyroid group of drugs) : These drugs have proved worthless in the long-run. In almost all the cases, the weight appeared to be increasing after the withdrawal of the drug. However, if it is conclusively diagnosed that the patient is suffering from hypothyrodism, these drugs can be administered cautiously. But such cases are very rare.

(4) Laxative drugs : These drugs act in the most unnatural and cruel way. They eliminate the food from the body, in the form of excretion, before it is absorbed in the intestines. The patient who takes these drugs becomes a victim of malnutrition; his gastrointestinal tract becomes weak and disorderly.

(5) Diuretics: These drugs drain off water and fluids from the body and create an illusion of weight-loss. They have proved to be absolutely useless in the long run.

The above discussion leads us to a conclusion that, barring some exceptional cases, use of these drugs is not desirable. They have more disadvantages than advantages. In the initial phase, these drugs appear to be working; but gradually their efficacy begins to wane. As a result of this, the patient is forced to increase their dosage and with that obviously the chances of side-effects also increase. It is a significant fact that in many developed and medically-advanced countries many 'Slimming Drugs' are banned.

Besides, it is an important fact that doctors also do not use these drugs for treatment of their own obesity. During the course of his survey of 832 doctors who had treated themselves for obesity, Dr. J. Yudkin observed that only 6.6% of them had used drugs![3]

It means that drugs are not a substitute of dieting or exercise. The root-cause of obesity is wrong habits of eating and living and these drugs do not even touch this cause in anyway.

Synopsis:

1. The use of drugs in the treatment of obesity is not desirable.
2. These drugs sometimes cause dangerous side-effects.
3. Even today, some of the drugs used in India for reducing weight are banned in the Western countries.
4. It is a significant fact that doctors themselves do not use drugs in the treatment of their own obesity.

References:

1. Dr. Bicknell (1952)–The Dietetic treatment of obesity, *Med. Press.* 19,11.
2. Jones, H. S. (1971)–Fenfluramine used as a substitute for methylamphetamines and dexamphetamines in the treatment of dependence on these drugs. *Suppl. to S.A. med. J., 19 June, p. 31.*
3. Yudkin, J. (1968)–Doctors' treatment of obesity, *Practitioner,* 201,330.

14. SURGERY IN THE TREATMENT OF OBESITY

Surgical experiments have also been carried out to perform surgery for reducing the excess fat.

There is a dental surgeon in Australia who performs an operation on molar teeth. He connects some of the lower molar teeth with their upper counter-parts with a metal wire. As a result of this, the patient's ability to open the mouth gets restricted. The opening is just adequate enough so as to allow only liquids to enter the mouth. Such a person is then given a daily diet of 800 calories in the form of milk, fruit-juices or other liquids.

Such a patient certainly loses some weight; but along with his weight, he loses something else also. For instance, he loses his ability to laugh heartily as he can't open his mouth sufficiently.

In another type of operation, some portion of the small intestine (and sometimes the entire small intestine) is cut and removed. Normally the food is digested in the stomach and the digested food is then absorbed in the small intestine. When the small intestine is removed, the absorption of the food is reduced and hence the body gets less amount of nutrition. Such an operation is called 'Intestinal-bypass surgery' or 'Jejuno-ileal shunt operation.'

The third type of surgery is known as 'cosmetic plastic surgery'. In it, layers of fat are removed by performing an operation on those parts of the body where the fat has accumulated (i.e., hips, breasts, thighs, stomach, etc.).

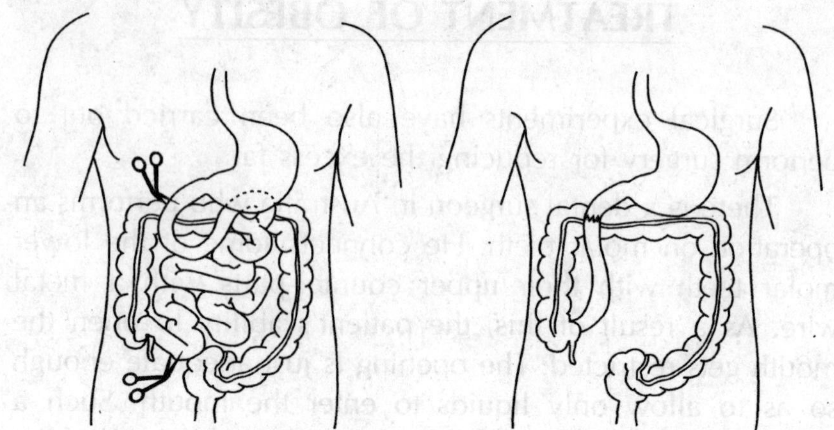

Fig. 54 : Surgery for removing some portion of the small intestine

All three types of operations certainly yield some positive gains, but that is to the doctor, not to the patient! The side-effects of the second type of surgery are so serious that the operation itself should only be considered impracticable. Here is a list of its side-effects: death on the operation table, infection in the wound, formation of stone in the kidney, osteoporosis, continuous nausea and vomitting, continuous diahorrea, distension of stomach, cirrhosis of liver, diseases caused by vitamin deficiency, hair-loss, arthritis, anaemia, etc. It is for these obvious reasons that this operation has never become popular. Most of the doctors too are against this operation.

Third type of surgery which is a local surgery for the removal of layers of fat is only a symptomatic treatment. It does not seek to eliminate or remedy the factors and the root-causes responsible for obesity. Though the fat is reduced for the time being, the factors and root-causes remain untouched and therefore the fat starts accumulating on the same parts of the body once again. But the incisions of the operation leave permanent scars on those parts of the body where surgery was performed.

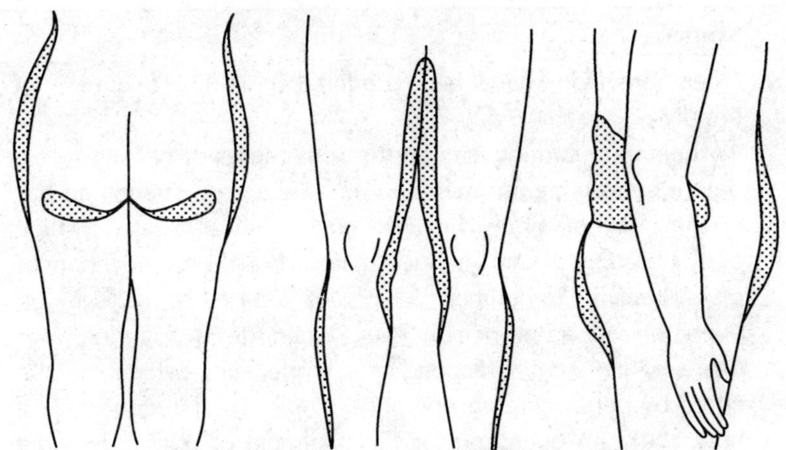

Fig. 55: Sites from where fat can be removed

In this context, there is yet another fact which calls for some thinking. In fat persons, vitality or resistance power is generally low. And under such circumstances, chances of developing inherent complications associated with surgery also increase. In cases of fat persons, post-operative progress is generally slow and it is an established fact that compared to normal persons the convalescence period of fat persons is always longer. In short, to lead a fat person to an operation table is to a certain extent a criminal act.

In fact, obesity is often an obstacle for other operations also. A doctor has to think several times before performing an operation on a fat person. It is extremely difficult to locate a particular part of the body or a nerve or a vein from the mass of fat. In this way in case of a fat person if a surgeon hesitates to perform other essential and life saving operations, it will be perfectly illogical to perform an operation for the treatment of obesity.

Synopsis:

1. Operations, too, have been undertaken in the treatment of obesity.
2. An operation cannot remove the root-causes of obesity.
3. Before performing an operation on a fat person, a surgeon has to think several times, because of the risk associated with it due to patient's low vitality, shallow breathing and chances of embolism. Sometimes, a surgeon refuses to perform an operation on a fat person even when he is suffering with diseases like hernia, appendicitis, stone, etc., which can be cured by performing an operation. Under such circumstances, how could an operation for the treatment of obesity be held logically acceptable?

Reference:

1. Bray. G. A. (1976)–The overweight patient, *Adv. Intern. Med.*, 21: 267.

15. ACUPRESSURE (REFLEXOLOGY) IN THE TREATMENT OF OBESITY

Acupressure and Acupuncture are oriental modes of treatment in which specific points on the skin are stimulated to favourably influence internal organs. While the required points are simply pressed in Acupressure, they are punctured (with needles) in Acupuncture.

These therapies originated almost 5000 years ago and they are being used even today. Thus, they have withstood the acid-test of time. This fact itself goes to prove their efficacy.

Presently, these therapies are being practised throughout the world. Even the WHO recognises these therapies as authentic and and effective modes of treatment and recommends their use in a variety of disorders and diseases.

While discussing the causes of obesity, we noted that, (1) a fat person's metabolism is slow, due to which the excess food he eats is not burnt away but is transformed into fat, (2) there is some malfunctioning in the digestive system of a fat person, due to which carbohydrate-metabolism stops after reaching a particular stage and (3) a fat person has voracious appetite which makes dieting very difficult for him.

Specific Acu-points which can be used to remedy these problems have been shown on the next page.

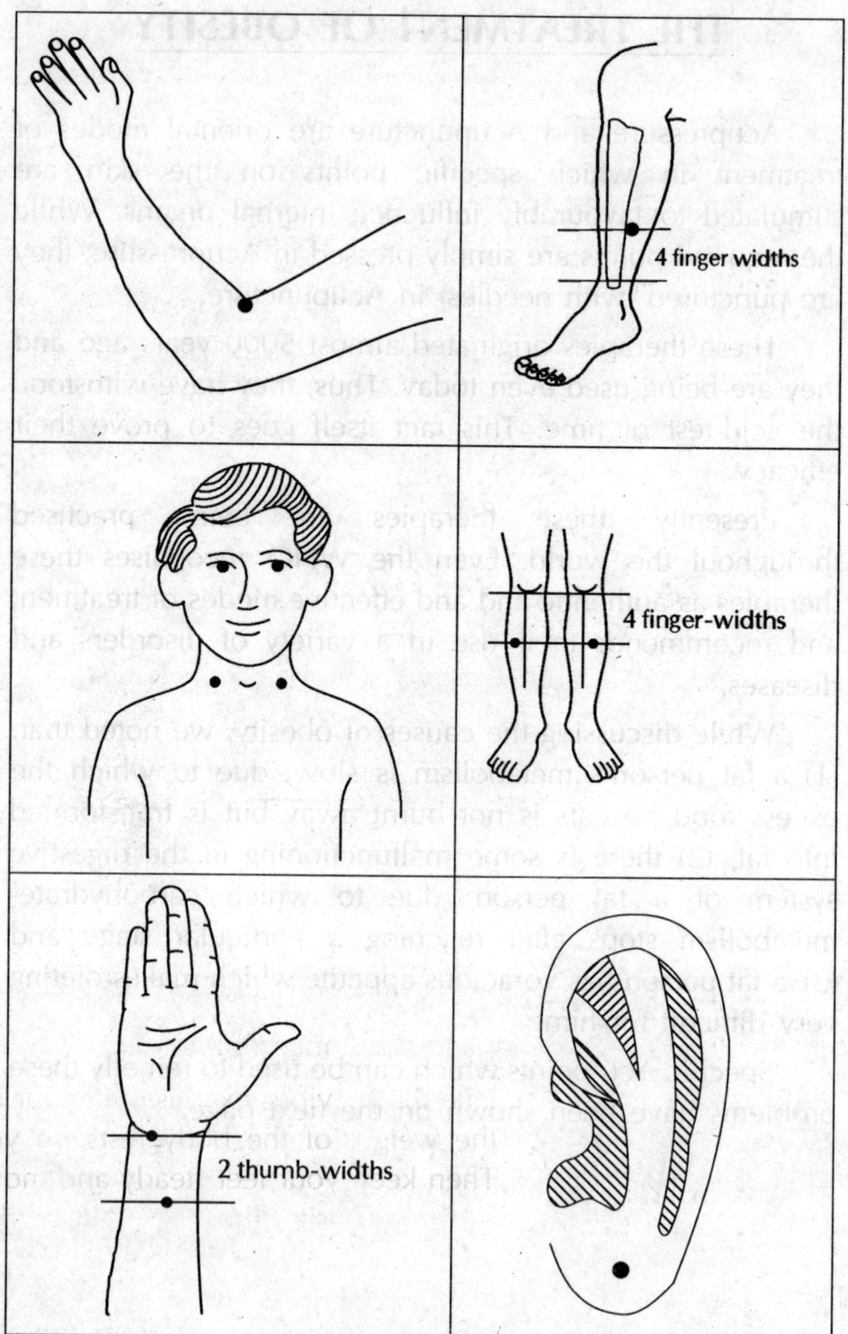

Fig. 56

Each of these points should be **deeply** pressed using the thumb or a finger or some blunt tool, for one minute in a pumping (press.. release... press... release) manner. The treatment should be carried out just before each meal. This results into a suppression of the appetite and a stepping up of metabolism.

Acupressure is entirely safe, unlike medicines and it costs nothing as it is a form of self-treatment. Detailed information about Acupressure has been given in the book 'Be Your Own Doctor With Acupressure' by the same authors.

16. MAGNET THERAPY IN THE TREATMENT OF OBESITY

Among modern therapies, magnet therapy also occupies a very important place. Hundreds of patients who are disappointed by the results of orthodox forms of treatment are now turning to the magnet therapy.

In this therapy, magnets are used for curing a patient's disease. Every magnet has two poles : North pole and South pole. When a magnet is tied to a string and suspended in the air, the end that points to the north is called the North pole and the end that points to the south is called the South pole. This is a universally accepted convention. Each pole has its own distinct characteristics. The South pole is cold and it slows down various processes of the body. The North pole is hot and it stimulates various processes of the body. The scope of magnet therapy science is very wide and here only a brief information can be given. (Further and extensive information on this subject is given in the book 'Magnet Therapy' by the same authors).

It is beyond doubt that in the war against obesity, the characteristic of the North pole, that it stimulates the processes of the body, is very useful. We have discussed earlier also that in a fat person's body, metabolism is slow and consequently the food, instead of being burnt away, gets transformed into fat. If the process of burning away the food can be stimulated in some way, the obesity can be prevented or removed.

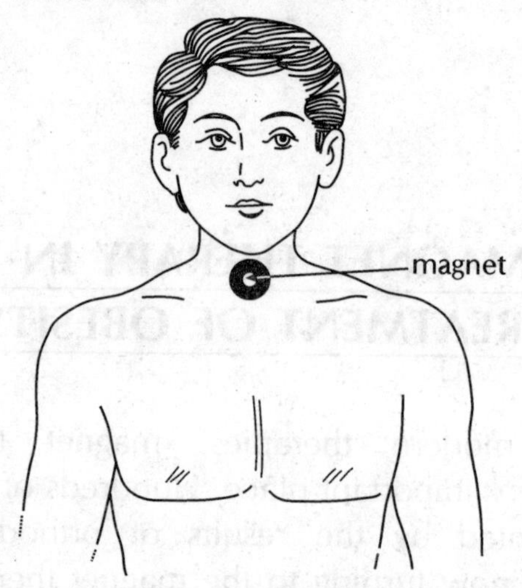

Fig. 57: Treatment of Thyroid gland with magnet

Metabolism of the body is directly related to the thyroid gland. If this gland, which is located at the base of the throat, is stimulated with a North pole, the basal metabolic rate goes up and the food is burnt in a larger quantity and that too faster. For this purpose, a fat person should keep the North pole of a medium powered (1500 to 2000 gauss) magnet at the base of the throat (see fig. 57) for about 15 minutes. This should be done twice or thrice a day after meals.

Besides this, he should drink 3 to 4 times during the day, the water treated with the North pole of the magnet. Each time the quantity of the water should be about half a cup.

Note: If a glass or a bottle filled with water is kept in constant contact with the North pole of a magnet, at least for twelve hours, it becomes properly magnetised (see fig. 58).

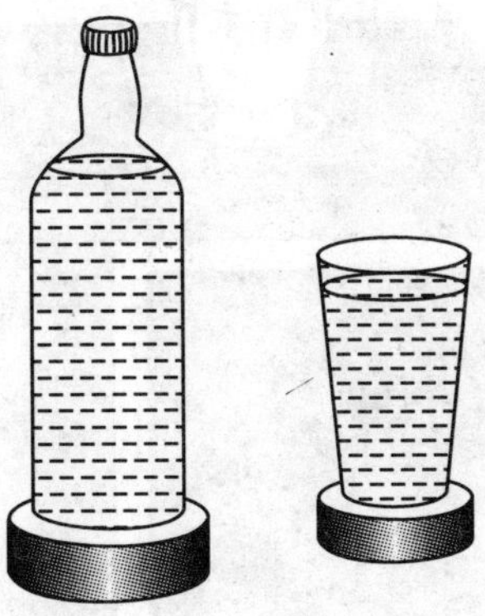

Fig. 58: Method to treat the water with magnet

Reference:

1. Dr. D. R. Gala, Dr. Dhiren Gala–Be Your Own Doctor With Magnet Therapy. *Navneet Publications (India) Ltd.*

17. SAUNA AND MASSAGE FOR LOSING EXCESS FAT

In the treatment of obesity experiments of **Sauna** and **Steam-bath** have also been popular. These experiments, though they may not yield a big gain, certainly cause no harm.

Fig. 59 : Steam-bath

This type of heat-treatment increases heat in the body and causes profuse perspiration. As a result of this, the basal metabolic rate goes up and health of the skin also improves.

Massage : In the treatment of obesity and for removing the excess fat from particular parts of the body, massage is used extensively. But it appears that its importance is slightly overemphasized in this regard.

However, if a person himself massages his body properly, it certainly does not cause any harm, but may yield some gains.

A person who massages his body himself gets enough exercise and consequently his excess calories are consumed. Besides this, massage improves the health of the skin. A person, who massages his body regularly need not worry about the possibility that after reduction in his weight, his skin might become flabby or that wrinkles might appear on it or that his skin would lose its lustre.

While massaging, care should be taken to ensure that the flow of the blood going towards the heart should be assisted and not vice versa. For instance, while massaging the arm, pressure should be applied in the direction from wrist to the elbow, but not from the elbow to the wrist.

18. HYPNOTISM IN THE TREATMENT OF OBESITY

As discussed earlier, causes of obesity include psychological factors and 'food addiction'.

Some people try to seek, in food, a solution to their psychological problems or adversities of life. Some others are not able to resist the temptation to eat tasty food in spite of the fact that they are fully aware that obesity is a dangerous disease. The treatment of obesity through hypnosis can be helpful to both these types of people.

Many psychiatrists resort to hypnotism in the treatment of obesity. First of all, the psychiatrist takes the fat patient into a deep trance (state of subconsciousness).

Thereafter, the person is given a post-hypnotic suggestion that after recovering from the trance (after recovering consciousness) his liking for sugar, biscuits, cake, sweets and other carbohydrates would disappear and his appetite would be reduced to some extent. The subconscious mind of the patient grasps those suggestions. After recovering from the hypnotic state when he goes home, he finds that he has developed an aversion for the above-mentioned carbohydrate foods. He is, thus, able to exercise dietary control easily and that helps him in reducing his weight.

This process of giving post-hypnotic suggestion has to be repeated from time to time. As long as the effect of the suggestions lasts, the patient has no problem in dieting. However, if the effect of the suggestions becomes too intense, sometimes the patient may develop an aversion to food altogether and this might lead him to starvation. However, such a situation generally does not arise.

But, it is more desirable that the patient himself faces his problems and tries to solve them. Dieting under the hypnotic suggestions is a passive act and the patient has no active participation in it.

However, in rare cases, where a patient is suffering from a psychological disorder or is unable to reduce his weight due to his weakness to resist the temptation to eat, hypnosis can be employed under the care of a proper expert. And it is only the expert who can decide in which case hypnosis is necessary and in which case it is not necessary.

FROM FAT TO FIT

SECTION 3

Some other important topics

19. The rate of weight-reduction
20. What if the weight is not reduced?
21. Maintaining the proper weight
22. Who should reduce weight and who should not?
23. Pregnancy and obesity
24. Childhood obesity
25. Sixteen practical suggestions
26. Some successful case histories

19. THE RATE OF WEIGHT-REDUCTION

In how many days will all my excess weight be reduced? In how many days will my body become proportionate? These are some of the questions which fat persons' doctors have to face frequently.

Human nature is indeed very strange. A person does not care for his body for a number of years and allows fat to accumulate. Then suddenly, he gets impatient and wants to get rid of those layers of fat overnight. He is generally not interested in reducing 4 to 5 kg in a month. He wants to achieve a miracle of reducing 8 to 10 kg in a month! Sometimes, an eligible girl wants to reduce 40 pounds of her weight in only a couple of months in order to find a suitable match for herself and get married!

The first thing that we have to bear in mind is that we have to discard only the excess fat from our body and protect other useful cells of the body and not become a victim of malnutrition.

It is indeed vey difficult to give an accurate estimate of the exact rate of weight-reduction.

In some cases, in the beginning, the amount of water and fluids in the body goes down quickly and therefore it appears that the weight is reducing fast. But after 3 or 4 days the rate of weight-reduction decreases.

The balance of the mineral sodium in the body also affects the rate of weight-reduction. Generally the carbohydrates keep under check, the process of elimination of sodium from the body. During the course of dieting, as the carbohydrate intake decreases, the sodium begins to get eliminated from the body. Along with itself, sodium eliminates water also from the body and consequently there is a rapid weight-loss. But afterwards when the elimination of sodium decreases, the rate of weight-reduction also decreases.[1]

In short, the high rate of weight-loss in the beginning is illusive. It slows down afterwards. However, this slow rate is maintained afterwards.

In the initial stage of dieting, those who live a sedentary life are generally advised to eat a 800 to 1,000 calorie food during the whole day and those who are engaged in the manual jobs are advised to take a 1,200 to 1,500 calorie food. The daily diet-plan suggested in Chapter **9** contains about 1,000 calories. Those who follow that diet-plan can hope to reduce about 4 to 12 pounds (2 to 5 kg) in about a month's time.

(**Note:** Readers are advised to consult appendices **1 and 2** given at the end of this book to calculate the calorific value of different foods.)

If a person is overweight by 30% or more, he should eat the food with a lesser amount of calories than suggested above. Similarly, if a person's weight is not reducing even after taking the suggested diet, it is obvious that he should impose a further cut in his diet.

Many cases are recorded wherein no adverse effect was noticed even when persons subsisted on a 400 to 450 calorie diet. However, such a drastic cut in the diet should be tried only in a hospital under proper medical supervision. Those who subsist on such a low-calorie diet should take vitamins and minerals in the synthetic form.

In conclusion, we have only to say that undue haste is not advisable in reducing the weight. Those who act with patience eventually succeed. In a long race, the sportsman generally runs at a slow and steady pace. If a person undertakes too rapid a weight-reduction programme, he may become a victim of complaints like anaemia, uneasiness, giddiness, etc. Those who reduce their weight at a miraculous pace generally find that the vitamin and mineral depots in their body are fast depleted.

Those who are suffering from heart disease; high blood pressure or diabetes are commonly advised to reduce their weight. Such people should never undertake a speedy weight-reduction programme.

We must bear in mind that weight has not to be reduced for some immediate or short term gain. Proper weight is a life-time necessity and therefore maintaining the reduced weight is more important than the rate of reducing the weight.

Synopsis:

1. It is difficult to give an exact estimate of the rate of weight-reduction.
2. Weight has not to be reduced for a short-term or immediate gain. It is a life-time necessity. And therefore, it is not advisable to reduce the weight with undue haste.

Reference:

1. Runcie, J. (1971)–Urinary Sodium and Potassium secretion in fasting obese subjects. *Br. med. J.*, ii, 2

20. WHAT IF THE WEIGHT IS NOT REDUCED?

Many people complain that their weight does not get reduced in spite of their sincere efforts. Some others say that their weight-reduction stops beyond a certain limit.

During the dietary regimen, a person undergoes a number of experiences. The rate of reduction is hardly ever constant or uniform. It varies from time to time. During the first two or three weeks, there is a rapid weight-loss; but afterwards the rate of weight-reduction slows down. This phase is known as the stagnation phase. Sometimes, this phase of stagnation may last for as long as two to three weeks.

The initial rapid weight-loss is due to the phenomenon of diuresis. But after a certain amount of water is eliminated from the body, the rate of weight-loss becomes extremely slow. During the phase of stagnation, salt and water retention occurs in the body. However after a few days, the process of diuresis commences on its own again and there is further reduction in the weight.

In case of women, accumulation of water in the body two or three days prior to menstruation is normal. It is likely that during this period there may not be any weight-loss. On the contrary, in some cases, there may be a slight weight-gain. Women should always bear this fact in mind.

The age-old experience is that people are always over-enthusiastic about any activity in the beginning but with the passage of time the enthusiasm cools down. This fact applies to the slimming programme also. Fat persons display great enthusiasm, care and anxiety in the beginning; but gradually their will-power starts weakening, the enthusiasm begins to wane and dieting is relaxed. When such developments occur, the rate of weight-loss slows down.

It is an established truth that most of the fat persons tend to overeat. They generally have a voracious appetite. During the dietary-regimen, their appetite causes uneasiness and agony for them. Sometimes, psychological factors are responsible for such an appetite. Many a time fat persons violate their dietary-regimen to satisfy their hunger.

In some cases, some psychological problem impairs the process of weight-loss. In such cases, there is no weight-loss unless that problem is solved with understanding.

If the rate of weight-loss is too slow, do the following:

(1) Enforce the dietary-regimen strictly. The uneasiness caused by dieting is always short-lived. In a few days, the body gets used to the low intake of food and with that the uneasiness also disappears. If the dietary-regimen is violated or interrupted frequently, the body can't adjust to the low intake of food; or at least it takes a very long time to get used to it. A small sacrifice made at the initial stage yields great benefits in the long run. Having ideal weight is like an insurance policy against the risk of developing dreadful diseases in later life.

(2) For three days, note down on a piece of paper all the food items that you happen to eat. Make a total of the calorific value of all the food items consumed by you during the three days. You will be surprised when you see the number of calories consumed by you. Experiments have shown that many a fat person derived inspiration from such a procedure of counting the calories. Till then they had been deceiving themselves about the bulk of their food intake.

(3) If you are suffering from some psychological problem, try to find a rational solution for the same. Sometimes, even an analysis of such a problem leads to weight-loss and such incidents are recorded where it has happened so. In serious cases, psycho-therapy or hypnosis can also help. Hypnosis can help a person in getting rid of his false hunger.

(4) However, if in spite of all these efforts, there is no weight-reduction, reduce the intake of sugar, salt and water. Take two or three times during the day, half a glass of warm water with a few drops of lemon added to it.

(5) If you continue to make efforts with patience and perseverance, there is no doubt about the fact that you will be able to reduce your weight.

Short-term fasting undertaken for reducing the weight has proved to be undesirable and ineffective. During the fasting-regimen, it is not only the fat that is destroyed, but some useful cells and organs of the body are also destroyed. In an experiment carried out by Dr. Benoit and his colleagues in 1965, it was observed that only 35% of the total weight-loss achieved during the fasting-regimen of 7 to 10 days was due to the elimination of fat. However, if the stubborn obesity does not yield to any other efforts, long-term fasting-regimen can be undertaken at a hospital under proper medical supervision.

In the context of the above discussion, it would be interesting to know about the case of Miss Lata. Lata (22) was a young, unmarried girl. To kill her time, she was doing her M.A. at St. Xavier's College, Bombay. She was severely overweight and wanted to reduce her weight. It was her contention that in her case there was no significant weight-loss in spite of her dieting and even fasting for some time.

Lata belonged to a wealthy family. The family had many servants and cooks. She was never required to walk as one of the cars was always at her disposal. She went in her car to college, market or even for buying vegetables.

Her past history was quite significant. When she was only seven, her mother expired soon after delivering a baby boy. Lata had taken great pains in bringing up her brother. After five years, her father married again. But Lata and her step-mother could not get along with each other. There was a conflict in the marital life of her father. The atmosphere of the house was always tense and disturbed. As a result of this, Lata tried to seek love and security in food. Till she attained the age of 17, she was slightly overweight, but soon afterwards, when her parents began to discuss proposals for her marriage, she started putting on weight!

Feeling ashamed of the fun poked at her by her friends, she tried, several times, to reduce her weight. But she had no success.

On making a detailed enquiry, she revealed that in the meals she took only a couple of chapatis. Thinking that one can eat fruits and vegetables as much as one wishes, she used to eat 3 to 4 bananas everyday. Besides this, she used to consume 3 to 4 bottles of soft drinks and a glass of fruit-juice also during the course of a day. Another significant fact in her case was the total lack of physical activity. She spent as many as 10 to 11 hours in sleeping.

In this way, psychological problem, lack of physical activity and excess calories consumed through soft drinks, all put together prevented her weight-loss.

I advised her to analyse her own case through the questionnaire given in chapter 8 of this book. She followed the advice and managed to achieve some weight-loss. But very soon her weight became stagnant.

Finally I advised her the following three measures:

(1) to consult a good psychiatrist.

(2) to increase activities involving physical exertion, for instance, she should walk a couple of miles everyday, she should go to college (which was not very far from her house) on foot, she should undertake skipping for about 15 to 20 minutes everyday and she should reduce hours of sleep.

(3) to stop consuming soft drinks and bananas altogether. I also asked her to maintain a record of all the foods and drinks consumed by her during the course of a day and find out the total calories consumed.

By maintaining such a record Lata realized that by consuming soft drinks and fruit-juice, she was adding 400 to 500 calories to her total food-intake!

After she undertook the above-mentioned programme, she began to lose weight at a satisfactory pace. Later on she developed interest in proposals of marriage also. A faster rate of weight-loss was achieved when the proposal of a suitable match for her was considered seriously!

21. MAINTAINING THE PROPER WEIGHT

The most common question that all fat persons always ask is: "Will I put on the lost weight once again?"

Sometimes, it does happen that the lost weight is regained after some time. Those people in whose case it happens that way always feel that inflation and recession of weight alternate in their life. Their life is like a lunar cycle. For some time their weight keeps on reducing. For a brief period, the reduced weight remains stable but after some time it once again starts increasing. In such cases, a thorough study of all the factors responsible for such a situation should be made.

Sometimes, weight is reduced for some specific purpose or for an immediate gain. And afterwards care is not taken to maintain it.

It is like this: Karodimal wants to invest in a life-insurance policy. But the Insurance Co. rejects his application as he is overweight. Karodimal starves himself, makes herculean efforts to reduce his weight and finally succeeds in reducing his weight. The Insurance Co. accepts his application. And from the very next day Karodimal starts putting on weight.

Komal is growing older day by day and has crossed the right age for marriage. But all those who come for an interview with her are scared away on seeing her obese body. Komal comes to know that after about a month, a son of her father's acquaintance is coming to India from abroad for getting married. Komal moves heaven and earth to reduce her weight. Fortunately the proposal materializes and Komal gets married. After a few days following the wedding, Komal's weight begins to increase.

Smt. Lalitadevi suspects that her handsome husband is attracted towards a young girl. She knows well that the reason for her husband's diminishing interest in her is her obese body. So, she joins one of the much-publicised and expensive slimming centres of the city. As she reduces her weight and regains her beauty, her husband returns to her. When she is convinced that everything is now alright, she again starts putting on weight.

In most of the cases, wherein the reduced weight starts increasing once again, it is the lack of will-power that is responsible for that development. Generally a slimming programme is launched with great enthusiasm and zeal; but with the passage of time, the enthusiasm begins to wane;

dietary restrictions are flouted one by one and consequently the weight starts increasing once again.

It is a sad fact that people are still not fully aware of the long-term hazards associated with obesity. In our society a fleshy body is a symbol of good health. When people happen to see a person who was slim once upon a time and had put on weight afterwards, they would soon drop a remark, "Oh, your health seems to have improved a lot!" Nobody realises that weight has nothing to do with good health. In the modern age, people are more interested in enjoying life and eating delicious dishes. People are fond of tasty varieties. Crowded stalls of Panipuri and Pavbhaji bear a witness to this fact. Even the newspapers publish regular columns supplying information regarding new dishes. It is high time, we came out of this world centred at the tongue and the belly. Let us bear in mind that all the happiness of life is not confined to food alone.

Follow the suggestions given below to maintain the weight-loss:

(1) It is true that once the weight is reduced and brought down to a desirable level, the food intake should be slightly increased. But it does not mean that it should be so increased that the weight starts increasing again.

(2) It is necessary to weigh yourself once a week to ensure that your weight continues to remain stable. Every time weigh yourself in the same type of clothes and footwear, at the same time of the day, preferably in the morning (soon after emptying your bowels and the urinary bladder).

It is also essential that the scale used for recording weight should also be the same every time. It is likely that the weight may vary during the course of a day; so fix the time and weigh yourself every time at the appointed hour only.

Maintain a record of your weight in a pro forma like the one given below:

	Date	Weight	Measurement of chest	Measurement of waist	Measurement of hips	Measurement of thighs
1						
2						

(3) Try to maintain your psychological balance too. Psychological factors play a vital role in causing obesity.

(4) Try to find out a rational solution to your problems and feelings of agony, depressions, worry, anger, etc. Do not try to suppress them by flying to food.

(5) Read carefully, twice a week, chapters 'Hazards of Obesity' and 'Gains of removing Obesity' given elsewhere in this book.

Synopsis:

1. 'Ideal weight' is a key to healthy life.
2. Read carefully, once or twice a week, the chapter 3 : 'Hazards of Obesity'.
3. Weigh yourself regularly at least twice a month.

22. WHO SHOULD REDUCE WEIGHT AND WHO SHOULD NOT?

Hazards and dangers of obesity are discussed in chapter 3. Barring a few exceptions, generally any reduction in the weight proves to be in the interest of a fat person.

Moderate obesity in the young and the middle-aged: Sometimes grave diseases caused by obesity cause a person's premature death. And that is the reason why it is essential that those who fall in this category should reduce their weight. If a person has a previous family history of high blood pressure or heart disease, it becomes all the more essential for him to reduce his weight. Similarly, if some abnormalities such as increased fasting blood sugar are detected, reduction in weight becomes imperative. Formerly a level of 260 to 300 mg% of cholesterol in the blood was considered to be normal; but modern researches and studies indicate that the weight-reduction is very essential if this level exceeds 220 mg%.

Severe obesity: Obesity-removal is a basic condition for maintaining the health of all those who are severely obese.

Obese children: It is difficult to remove obesity from the body once it gets established. And therefore, it is advisable to take proper care of all those children who are becoming obese from their very childhood. Mothers of such children should acquire complete information regarding balanced diet and should take care to ensure that their children cultivate the right habits of eating and living.

It is advisable to undertake the obesity-removal programme cautiously or under proper medical care in the following circumstances:

(1) When the patient is suffering from some grave or serious disease.

(2) Those patients who are suffering from peptic ulcers should get the ulcer treated first.

(3) It is desirable that the treatment of obesity should not be launched (or launched under proper medical care) till a patient is cured, or relieved to some extent, from the following disease(s):

Liver disorders, gout, cancer, high diabetes, etc.

(4) Those who are suffering from low-blood pressure should also reduce their weight carefully. They should not make haste. Such persons should go about carefully in the matters of low-calorie diet and heavy exercises.

(5) Some people develop hypoglycemia soon after they start dieting. This trouble develops gradually. Its symptoms are : profuse sweating, paleness of skin, numbness in hands and feet, rigors, acute hunger, strange sensations in the head, fast pulse-rate, palpitation and unconsciousness. Such people should beware of the above-mentioned symptoms. If such symptoms appear, they should increase the amount of carbohydrate-intake in their food. Such symptoms also begin to disappear if a person takes a sweet drink. However, it must be borne in mind that such cases are very rare.

(6) Patience is essential while reducing obesity in the old age.

Barring the above-mentioned circumstances, there is no harm in launching a rigorous obesity-removal programme. In the above-mentioned cases too, weight-reduction would prove beneficial; albeit, it should be undertaken cautiously, patiently and under proper medical supervision.

23. PREGNANCY AND OBESITY

While giving a history of their obesity, 50% of women say that their weight has increased during and after pregnancy. What then is the relationship between pregnancy and obesity? Is it inevitable that there should be a weight-gain during and after pregnancy? It is necessary to discuss these questions in detail because abnormal weight-gain creates problems for both – the mother and the foetus.

How much weight-gain is normal during pregnancy?: Extensive studies have been made on this subject as to find out how much weight-gain is normal during pregnancy. An analysis of the date and figures collected from our country indicates that a weight gain of 8 to 10 kg (17.5 to 22 pounds) during pregnancy is normal.

Given in the table[1] below is an analysis of the weight-gain:

Factor	Average weight increase	
	in kg.	in lb.
1. Foetus	3.4	7.5
2. Placenta	0.65	1.4
3. Liquor amnii	0.8	1.8
4. Uterus	0.97	2.2
5. Breasts	0.4	0.9
6. Blood (increase in volume)	1.25	2.7
7. Extracellular fluid	1.68	3.7
Besides, there is a slight weight-gain due to increase in total body-fat.		

Generally the weight should come down to its normal level soon after the delivery. But in cases of some women, it does not happen that way. Their weight starts increasing during pregnancy and there is no significant weight-loss after pregnancy. Many factors could be responsible for such a phenomenon. Sometimes, a pregnant woman is over-fed under the false notion of providing double nutrition–to the mother and to the child. Many a time, a pregnant woman is not allowed to do any physical work. Lack of physical activity and overeating–these two factors are generally responsible for the abnormal weight-gain during pregnancy. Sometimes, when a woman returns home from the maternity home, she is given a lot of unnecessary food such as, saubhagya-sunthipak, methipak, badam-shira, sweets, dry fruits, etc. As a result of that, layers of fat accumulate on her body.

Care should be taken to ensure that the weight-gain does not exceed the level indicated in the above table. For this, an expectant mother should be weighed regularly every month during the first six months of her pregnancy and every fortnight thereafter. Care should also be taken to ensure that there is no weight-gain beyond 2 kg on an average, every month.

Hazards of excessive weight-gain:

(1) Effect on the expectant mother: Excessive food intake during pregnancy increases the weight which in turn

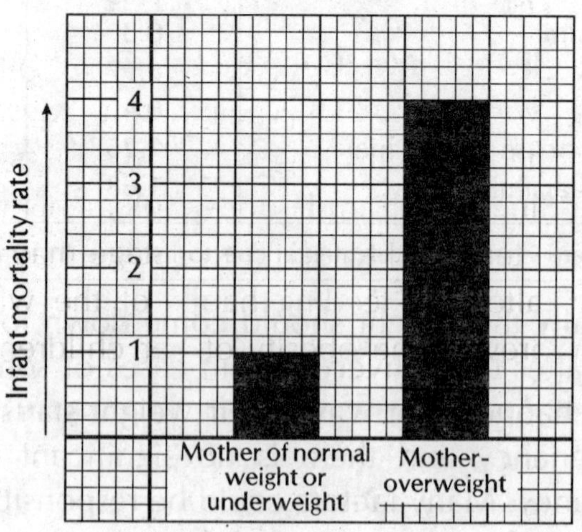

Fig. 60

may cause grave consequences. After studying the cases of 641 obese women, Dr. Odel and Dr. Mangerton observed that in cases of obese pregnant women, the incidence of toxaemia of pregnancy[2], mallocation of foetus, unbearable pain and post-natal bleeding is very high. Obese women generally do not have normal deliveries. Either a forceps delivery or a Caesarean operation is required. Besides this, the mother's life is generally in danger for a few days following the delivery. Those women who have a family history of diabetes, heart-disease or obesity need to take extra precautions during their pregnancy. Being underweight prior to conception is no guarantee that obesity will not develop during pregnancy. On the other hand, obesity at the onset of pregnancy gives rise to an increased risk of developing complications mentioned earlier.

(2) Effect on the foetus: Maternal obesity increases the risk of foetal-mortality by about 4 times.[3, 4]

If the mother is obese during pregnancy, the chances of injury to the tender limbs of the foetus during the delivery are also enhanced.

Why is dietary advice necessary during pregnancy?: Generally a woman develops health-consciousness during pregnancy. She generally accepts all the suggestions and advice regarding health and soon implements them. Right dietary advice tendered to her at this stage may help her to permanently alter the feeding habits of the whole family and thereby prevent the obesity of her children also.

Aims of dietary-control during pregnancy:

(1) To check undue weight-gain.

(2) To maintain the health of mother and child.

(3) Proper development of foetus.

The following diet-plan is recommended to fulfil the above-mentioned goals:

(1) Take high-protein foods.

(2) Restrict the intake of carbohydrates and fats.

(3) Increase the intake of raw vegetables and fruits so as to supply vitamins and organic minerals to the body.

(4) Restrict the intake of salt.

What should be consumed and what should be avoided?:

(1) Restrict the use of ghee, butter, bread, biscuits, cake, sugar, chocolates, sweets, rice, etc.

(2) There is no harm in consuming the following items freely:

grains (ground or pounded by hands), vegetables, fruits, milk, buttermilk, curd, etc.

If a pregnant woman gives up her habit of eating too often, does all the household chores, goes for a walk in the open air or does any light physical work and prevents obesity, she does not need to worry about any untoward incident during pregnancy or at the time of delivery.

Synopsis:

1. The weight gain during pregnancy should not exceed 8 to 10 kg.
2. When a woman is forced to take unnecessary rest and consume a rich diet during and after pregnancy, she develops obesity.
3. Obesity creates danger to the life of both–mother as well as the child.

References:

1. Hytten, F. E. & Leitch, J. (1969)– *The Physiology of Human Pregnancy,* 2nd edition, Blackwell, Oxford.

2. **Note:** Toxaemia of pregnancy is a grave condition dangerous to the life of an expectant mother. There can be two reasons for weight-gain during pregnancy: (1) Accumulation of fat and (2) retention of water. The problem of toxaemia is associated with the latter. If there is a sudden weight-gain in the last trimester of pregnancy coupled with high blood pressure, it could be a symptom of toxaemia. In this critical illness, patient is advised to consume salt-free and low-carbohydrate-diet. It is imperative to consult a qualified gynaecologist for the treatment of this problem.
3. Richardson, J. S. (1952)–The treatment of maternal obesity, *Lancet,* ii, 550.
4. Sheldon, J. H. (1949)–Maternal obesity. *Lancet,* ii, 869.

24. CHILDHOOD OBESITY

Sometimes, childhood obesity is treated as a separate problem, independent from adult obesity. Some experts have enumerated independent causes for childhood obesity and have recommended a different treatment for the same.

Although it is true that some changes are required in the treatment of childhood obesity, however, the basic principles underlying the treatment of adults as well as children remain the same. The changes which are called for are due to the factor of physical growth in children.

Causes behind childhood obesity: In our social environment, some undesirable traditions have taken roots. Due to them children are prone to treat food not only as a means to satisfy hunger, but also as a means of entertainment or enjoyment. A child feels as if human life is meant only for enjoying food! Sometimes, the child is denied food as a mark of punishment, and at other times some rich food is offered to him as a reward for some good behaviour. In this way, the seeds of 'comfort eating' are sown from the very childhood. Crying is a frequent activity of a little child. More often than not, he cries because he is hungry. But sometimes, he cries just to draw his parent's attention or when he needs their affectionate touch. But instead of getting what he wants, what he gets every time is a bottle of milk. And what is surprising is that when he gets the bottle, he stops crying and feels happy. Can a bottle of milk be a substitute for natural love and affection? Such a thing should not happen. But the fact remains that it happens that way. Gradually the child gets used to this ploy. But then, whenever he needs natural love and affection he demands food. This habit continues thereafter, albeit in a slightly different form, even when he grows up. State of mental tension, anger or anxiety invariably leads him to food-tins. Once this false notion takes deep roots in the child's mind he seeks, throughout his life, solutions to his psychological problems, disappointments, sense of insecurity, etc. in food only. Food acts like a drug for suppressing mental tension, anxiety, excitement, etc. The weight and the fat may increase gradually at a later age; but their seeds are sown earlier in the mind of that person during his childhood.

Generally children and parents take meals together. It is a well-known fact that wrong habits of eating and living are also sometimes responsible for causing obesity. A child usually imitates parents' habits and imbibes their wrong habits quickly.

Lack of adequate physical activity also plays a major role in causing obesity in childhood. Sometimes, parents and servants make the child dependent on them. They don't allow him to play freely for the fear that he would get hurt or that he would be ill or that the children of the neighbourhood would spoil him. Lack of encouragement prevents the child from participating in the sports activities at the school also. This lack of adequate physical activity later on manifests its results through the accumulation of layers of fat in the body. As obesity keeps on increasing the physical activity of the child keeps on decreasing.

Genetic factors in childhood obesity: Some experts accept the importance of genetic factors in childhood obesity; while there are some others who reject them altogether.

Extensive studies indicate that only 9 % of the children become obese if their parents are of normal weight. If either of the parents is overweight, 50 % of their children tend to become obese. However, if both the parents are overweight the percentage of fat children touches the figure of 80.

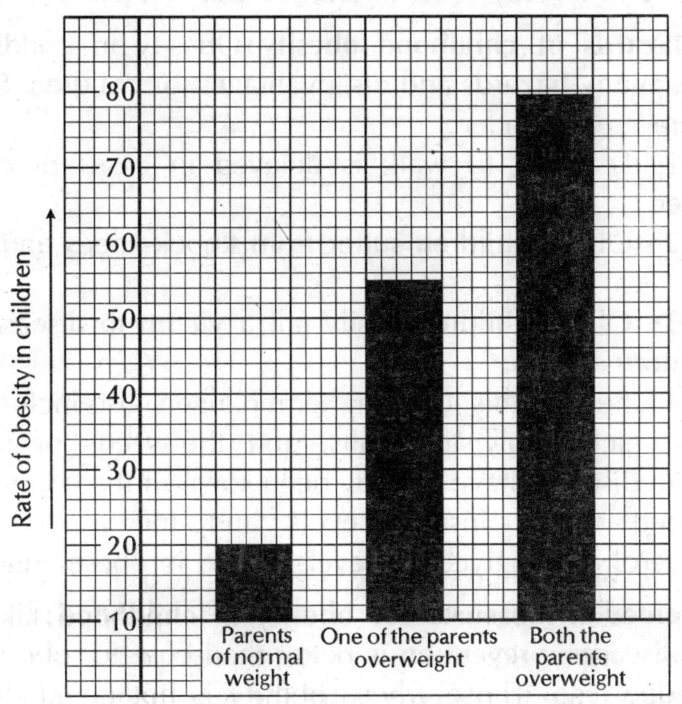

Fig. 61

Dr. Gene Mayor, who has studied this subject in depth, says that a child inherits from his parents only the body-frame and not obesity. Children are never born obese; they are made obese.

It is now established conclusively that endocrine gland disorders are also not responsible for obesity in childhood.

Dr. Talbot[1] emphatically says, "95 out of every 100 fat children become obese due to their tendency to overeat."

Dr. Bruch[2], who has studied the case of obese children carefully, says that such children attain physical maturity earlier compared to normal children. Obese girls start menstruating earlier. In short, in the matters of physical growth, obese children are ahead of normal children by several years. Excessive food intake affects the physical growth and obesity is its natural consequence.

Hazards of childhood obesity: Obesity in childhood creates many hazards and disadvantages for children. Some of them are as under:

(1) Learning to walk is delayed in cases of obese children.

(2) Obese children suffer from knock-knees and flat-feet.

(3) Obese children easily fall a victim to diseases of respiratory system.[3]

(4) Besides this, the long-term dangers also include all those which apply to adults, and the seeds of future dreadful diseases have already been sown in the commonly increased serum insulin levels and increased serum cholesterol and triglyceride levels, found in obese children.

Remedial measures for obesity in childhood: Like all other diseases, prevention is better than cure for obesity in childhood also. Those whose obesity is not cured during childhood find it very difficult to reduce their weight at a later age.

Prevention of obesity: (1) Breast-fed babies are less likely to become obese. During the course of his study, Dr. Taitz[4] observed that only 4 out of 21 of breast-fed babies were overweight as compared to 143 out of 240 of bottle-fed babies.

(2) During childhood, cultivating right eating habits is of paramount importance. A child's diet should be well-balanced. To fulfil this requirement the whole family should examine their eating habits. Do not allow the child to become an addict of carbohydrate-foods such as sweets, soft drinks, chocolates, biscuits, cake, ice cream, etc. Do not force him to eat if he is not willing to eat. That woman is a lucky mother who complains that her child forgets to eat his food when he is engrossed in some other activity or games.

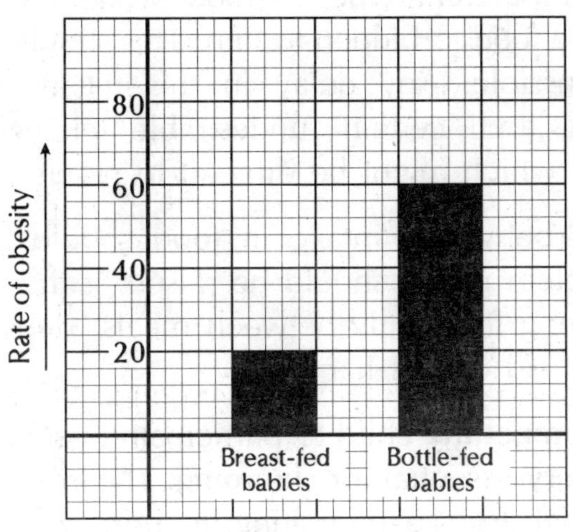

Fig. 62

(3) Encourage the child to participate in sports and other physical activities. Do not make him a home-keeping bird.

(4) Try to satisfy your child's psychological needs also. He needs your warmth, affection and love. The sense of security derived from them plays a vital role in preventing obesity.

How to remove childhood obesity? : Any planning for a slimming-programme for children demands deep understanding, tact and patience. For a child, the intake of food is a major source of happiness. Dieting means a direct cut in this happiness. And therefore in any dietary control, the child's complete and whole-hearted co-operation is very essential. So, keeping in view of the above facts, the following remedial measures may be taken:

(1) Review the atmosphere of mental peace prevailing in the home. If necessary, make suitable changes in it.

(2) It is essential that the whole family should change their eating and living habits. It is not possible that the child alone takes different type of food while others happily consume the food forbidden to him. This should be done as early as possible. Any delay in this regard may cause weight-gain and certain undesirable changes in the metabolism which might be difficult to reverse afterwards.

The carbohydrate intake in food should be reduced and the protein intake should be raised. If the child has a habit of eating frequently between meals, steps should be taken to get rid of that habit.

(3) Compel the child to participate in sports. Physical activity is very essential for slimming. The child can derive a great benefit from participating in sports and from going for long walks in the fresh air. It is essential that physical activity should be done daily and regularly.

(4) It is not desirable to impose a big cut on obese children's diet. In this regard, the treatment of children's obesity differs from that of the adults. It is unnecessary to make any efforts to actually reduce children's weight. It is enough to devise a diet-plan that ensures prevention of weight-gain. As the child grows, he gradually moves towards his ideal weight. It is also necessary to insure that during his dietary-regimen, he gets an adequate supply of vitamins and minerals.

Synopsis:

1. If the parents are obese, the chances of their children becoming obese are high.
2. A child becomes obese if he is deprived of breastfeeding, is over-fed or is not allowed to participate freely in sports and other physical activities.
3. If the atmosphere in the home is not peaceful, the child flies to food for comfort and in turn becomes obese.
4. Obesity creates many hazards for a child.
5. It is not desirable to impose a big dietary cut in the treatment of obesity in childhood. A child should be given enough food so as to maintain his existent weight. As the child grows, he moves towards his ideal weight.

References:

1. Talbot, N. B. (1945)–Obesity in children, *M. Clin. N. America*, 29:1217.
2. Bruch, H. (1939)–Obesity in childhood–I Physical growth and development of obese children, *Am. J. Dis. Child:,* 58:457.
3. Hutchinson-Smith, B. (1970)–The relationship between the weight of an infant and lower respiratory tract infections, *Med. Off*, 123, 257.
4. Taitz, L. F. (1971)–Infantile over-nutrition among artificially-fed infants in the Sheffield region, *Bri. Med. J.*, i, 315.

25. SIXTEEN PRACTICAL SUGGESTIONS

(1) Do not be over-enthusiastic in the slimming programme. Do not starve yourself. The fat that has accumulated over a period of years becomes a part of the body and it is not desirable to make any undue haste in trying to get rid of it. Weight-reduction programme should be undertaken rationally and in a planned manner. Those who do not use discretion in the treatment of their obesity sometimes land up into difficulties.

(2) Although we have already had a discussion earlier in this book as to what the fat people should eat and what they should avoid, let us repeat some points in this regard as they are of vital importance. Following is the list of forbidden foods for fat people.

Forbidden Foods:
Cake, biscuits, ice cream
Dry fruits
Potatoes, edible roots (tubers)
Soft drinks and fruit juices
Alcohol

Note: It is desirable that these forbidden foods are not stored in the home at all.

Following foods are freely allowed:
Vegetable salad
Vegetable soup or Moong soup (flour not to be used for making the soup.)

Note: Take before meals, a glass of diluted buttermilk with ice added to it.

(3) There is no need to harbour a false notion that you can eat only boiled items during dieting. Tastefulness is the essence of meals. If the food is tasteless, you are bound to develop an aversion for it in a few days. So, do maintain a variety in your food items. Add spices to them on a moderate scale. But restrict the use of salt.

(4) Stop using a big plate. Use a small dish or a plate for your meals.

(5) Cut the raw vegetables and ingredients of salad yourself while you have your meals. Make small pieces of chapati or khakharas.

(6) Take small morsels. Chew the food properly. Chew every morsel at least 15 times so that the food is turned into liquid form. Remember the adage : 'Do not eat your food; drink it'.

(7) Keep an interval of about 15 seconds between morsels of food while you are taking your meals.

(8) Fix a particular place for eating meals (for example : kitchen) and stick to it.

(9) It is experts' opinion that fat persons should not eat more than thrice a day. So plan your food intake in such a way that your total food intake is equally distributed in three sessions. It is not desirable to make one of the meals heavier and the other a lighter one. It has been proved through experiments, that the chances of reduction in weight decrease if a person eats a big meal in a single session. You should not eat anything between your meals.

(10) If unbearable hunger develops between two meals, it can be satisfied by taking low-calorie food items. Keep items like carrots and cucumber always at hand. Such items do not contain high-calorific value and yet they give a person the feeling of satiety. To satisfy the hunger one can also take a glass of water with a few drops of lemon added to it.

(11) Despite eating above-mentioned items, if the hunger keeps on bothering you, go for a walk in the fresh air or do some light exercise followed by a hot-water bath.

(12) It is desirable to take your dinner as early as possible so that you have an hour or two to spare and then go for a walk covering a distance of about 1 to 1.5 km. Those who do not do any other exercise should go for a similar walk in the early morning also.

(13) Take care of the psychological factors at work during the dieting. Human mind is both, strange and fickle. It always craves for that which is not available. In the initial

stages of dieting, first one or two weeks pose a challenge to the obese person. Temptation to eat tasty food becomes very strong. At this juncture great amount of patience and firmness are required. Sometimes, symptoms like weakness, headache, insomnia and acidity also develop. But do not lose heart. Meet the challenge bravely. Once you cross this critical stage, things will be easy for you.

(14) Sometimes, a person who is on a dietary-regimen or on a fasting-regimen develops acidity. As a result of this, he develops headache, bodyache, nausea, vomitting, etc. When such symptoms occur, some patients are frightened and give up the regimen.

During the course of dieting carbohydrate-intake is reduced drastically and consequently the fat accumulated in the body begins to dissolve. This causes ketosis which is responsible for causing the above-mentioned complaints. Ketosis can be avoided and relief from the above-complaints can be obtained by consuming large quantities of vegetables, fruits, coconut water, etc.

You need not worry even if hyper-acidity develops occasionally. If you deal with it patiently, it will subside in a few days.

(15) Keep yourself busy and occupied during the critical phase. Do not think of food. Do not discuss food with anyone during those days. Avoid handling food-containers during those days. Do not go to market for buying foodstuffs.

(16) Sometimes, an inadvertant breach occurs in the dietary-regimen. You may yield to the temptation of eating a forbidden food item. After such a lapse, a person generally feels disturbed or suffers from the guilt-feeling. It is likely that he would be swept off his feet by the spell of

depression and abandon the dieting altogether. Therefore, psychologists say that it is necessary to prepare the patient mentally for the dieting and make necessary changes in his attitude also. The following comparison gives an idea about the distinction between proper attitude and self-deceptive attitude :

Self-deception	Proper attitude
1. Now that I have already eaten the Halwa and thereby broken the rules of dieting I should give up dieting altogether.	It doesn't matter even if I have eaten some Halwa. I can still compensate for the damage done. I'll cut the consumption of some other food item and will not exceed the total stipulated consumption of the calories.
2. I swear that now onwards I'll never eat Halwa and will do the exercise regularly.	No human being is perfect. I'll be careful not to repeat such a mistake.
3. I don't have any will-power as I can't resist any temptation.	I am progressing. I need not be disappointed by the obstacles. It takes some time to change old habits.
4. Slim persons are lucky people. They can eat what they like.	Slim people have their own problems. It's of no use envying them.

26. SOME SUCCESSFUL CASE HISTORIES

Note: Real names of the patients referred to in these case histories have not been revealed to protect their identities.

①

Nayana Parekh was a young lady of 29. She had a fair complexion. She also possessed a beautiful face and hazel eyes. But obesity was marring the beauty of her body. Due to her obesity, she had not been able to find a suitable match. Many suitors came to see her, but none was prepared to accept her as life-partner. Nayana was, therefore, very unhappy. Members of her family were also worried about her.

Nayana belonged to a Jain family. So, she was accustomed to occasional fasts. During the last 'Paryushana' festival, she had undertaken an eight-day fast too. As a result of this, she had lost some weight. But soon afterwards, she had gained her lost weight. She had tried several remedies to reduce her obesity but all her attempts had been in vain.

One day, she came to me for treatment. At that time her weight was 70 kg. Her height was 5′ 2″. As she had a narrow frame, she was overweight by about 25%. She wished to undertake long-term fasting under my supervision. But I explained to her that her obesity was a result of faulty habits of eating and living coupled with lack of physical activity. I also explained to her that it was not desirable to remove obesity through fasting. The right remedy for her was to cultivate proper habits of eating and living.

I recommended her an 800 calorie-diet and gave her a chart for the same. I also instructed her to do some skipping and go for a brisk walk early in the morning. I sent her away advising her to see me twice a week.

Nayana was fond of spicy food and tasty dishes. So, in the beginning for a couple of days, she found it very difficult to subsist on`the diet recommended by me. But she remained firm and got used to it. After $2\frac{1}{2}$ months, she had reduced 13 kg. She was quite happy as her weight was normal keeping in view her height and frame.

Thereafter I permitted her to slightly increase her food intake so as to maintain her weight. I also instructed her to get herself weighed twice every week.

After about three months, when Nayana came to see me, her weight was 55 kg. She handed over her wedding invitation to me and said that correct habits of eating and living had become an Integral part of her life.

I too assured her that if she lived like that her weight would never increase in future.

(2)

Dinesh Jani, aged 35, was an insurance agent. Once he participated in an international competition and as luck would have it, he won the contest! He was awarded a free return ticket to Singapore and Bangkok. He was scheduled to leave after about a month.

Though he had got the prize, Dinesh found himself between two horns of dilemma. In the last few years, he had put on a lot of weight. When he walked, his thighs rubbed against one another. At the slightest exertion, he got breathless and his heartbeats also increased. He was forced to take some rest before resuming work. Under such conditions, he wondered how he could undertake a journey abroad.

Dinesh knew me well. So he came to me and explained his problem. I apprised him of the hazards associated with obesity and said that to remain healthy normal weight was essential throughout one's life. But at that time, he was only interested in losing his weight very fast. He wanted to reduce his weight from 75 kg to 60 kg in just three weeks. He was not interested in reducing his weight gradually.

Considering his predicament, I prescribed a 400 calorie-diet for him. Coupled with it were vitamin tablets, sauna-bath, magnet therapy and exercises. As he remained at home for most of the time during day, he did not find it difficult to implement the above package.

As his weight began to decrease, his breathing became regular. He felt energetic and fit as his body became light. He achieved his target of the weight-loss in just about three weeks. In the last week, I allowed him a slight increase in the food intake. At the end of four weeks, his programme also came to an end and he was able to proceed happily to Singapore.

③

When Mr. Hasmukh Shah called on me, he appeared to be in a frightened and worried state.

He was severely overweight. But I made no reference to that and asked him about the cause of his anxiety. In reply, he told me that his family physician had put him on Flabolin (Fenfluramine) – a slimming drug-two months ago. His weight had started reducing slowly. But along with that his hours of sleep had also decreased. But it did not occur to him that it was that drug which was responsible for his reduced hours of sleep. Thereafter since last four days, he had developed severe colic pain, diarrhoea, heaviness in the chest, dry throat and some other complaints. When he had phoned his family-physician and told him about these complaints, he asked him to withdraw that drug forthwith.

Hasmukhbhai was very fond of food. And therefore, he had resorted to drug therapy for reducing his weight. But now he had realized the dreadfulness of those drugs and he had come to me rushing. His weight was 90 kg. According to his height, his weight should not have been more than 60 kg. So, he was overweight by about 33 %. I explained to him that safety lay in reducing the weight gradually and prescribed for him an 800 to 1,000 calorie-diet. As his blood-pressure was normal, I also advised him to go for jogging in the morning.

After about a month, as there was no significant change in his weight, I imposed a further cut on his diet. Still, after about a fortnight, there was no reduction in his weight. I was surprised. On making enquiries, I learnt that Hasmukhbhai had yielded to temptations several times during the dietary-regimen. He admitted that he had not been able to adhere strictly to the prescribed diet.

So I advised him to do the following:

(1) He should use saccharin instead of sugar.

(2) He should eat 3 to 4 cucumbers before meals. He should peel the cucumbers himself. He should then make small pieces of them and eat them one by one. He should chew each piece at least 10 to 12 times. He should spend at least 10 minutes in eating them. Thereafter, he should chew every morsel of food during the meal in a similar manner. He should take a few sips of water after every 3 to 4 morsels.

(3) If he felt hungry between two meals, he should eat cucumbers, carrots, radishes or tomatoes.

(4) He should maintain a record of all the food items consumed by him during the whole day.

(5) He should go for a walk early in the morning and in the evening after dinner. He should cover a distance of at least 1 to $1\frac{1}{2}$ miles during those walks.

(6) He should get himself weighed every third day.

I gave him strict instructions to follow the programme sincerely. At last, the experiment met with due success. There was a rapid reduction in Hasmukhbhai's weight. As his weight began to reduce, his sincerity and enthusiasm began to increase. He slowly began to cover longer distances in his walks also. At the end of four months, his weight stood at 65 kg.

Miss Susan D'Souza was a successful model by profession. She figured in many prominent ads appearing in popular magazines and journals. She earned a handsome remuneration from her profession. And therefore, there were frequent parties and friendly get-togethers. As a result, Susan's weight began to increase.

In the beginning, Susan ignored her weight-gain. She thought it was a good sign. But realization dawned upon her when advertising agencies began hiring other models to replace her. She got worried and began to make attempts, on, to reduce her weight. But her attempts did not produce any encouraging results. It appeared that her weight was reducing for a while, but she would again put on weight. As Susan was an educated girl, she had read about surgery to remove excess fat. So she began to enquire about a competent surgeon.

It was around that time that one of her friends brought her to me. Susan appeared very anxious to reduce her weight as she wanted to regain her modelling contracts.

I explained to her the futility of surgery in reducing weight. I asked her not to get panicky and also explained to her that by reducing the weight gradually she would be able to maintain her health properly and there would be no changes in the beauty of her complexion as well as her face.

It was easy to prescribe a high-protein diet for her as she was a non-vegetarian. I issued her strict instructions to refrain from consuming items like cold beverages, ice-cream, bread, cake, biscuits, etc. I suggested to her a few exercises to make her limbs shapely and also asked her to do some massage to retain the lustre of complexion. Susan showed willingness to see me every alternate day.

But, even after four days, there was no significant change in her weight. Her period of stagnation continued for quite sometime. So I imposed a further cut on her diet and asked her to reduce her salt-intake. From the fifth day, her weight began to reduce. As her weight began to reduce, her enthusiasm began to increase. She even decided voluntarily to wave the liberties she had earlier taken in the dietary-regimen. Gradually exercises were also increased. During the entire course of treatment, Susan's enthusiasm and co-operation remained noteworthy.

After some time when her weight was reduced to normal she once again started getting offers for modelling.

(5)

Smt. Jayaben Pandya was happy in every respect except for the fact that she had no children. She had tried several remedies, had taken many drugs and medicines but everything had been in vain. Reports revealed that her husband was also not suffering from any deficiency. Finally, doctors advised her to reduce her weight.

Jayaben's husband brought her to me. Jayaben who was 5′-2′ tall weighed 65 kg. There were layers of fat on her waist and arms. Her diet had been a typical Gujarati family fare. Morning breakfast consisted of two cups of tea with items like puri, sevchivda, etc. Vegetables cooked in abundant oil, chapatis, with ghee generously applied on them and large quantity of rice were some of the items of lunch. Evening tea was also taken with some snacks and she concluded her day with a supper consisting of items like khichdi or bhakhari. 3 to 4 times in a week, fried dishes were also a part of the supper. Jayaben was very social and used to take snacks offered to her during her social visits to relatives and acquaintances. It would have been surprising had such a diet not caused accumulation of fat in the body.

I prepared a diet-chart for Jayaben. I advised her to take one cup of tea with saccharin added to it in the morning, chapatis without applying ghee on them, boiled vegetables, and a large quantity of green salad during the meals. I also suggested to her that she should do certain household chores herself.

These efforts produced the desired result. In about three months' time, her weight was reduced to 50 kg. I then allowed her a slight increase in the food-intake and also permitted her to add some spices to her food. She used to call on me for a health check-up quite frequently.

After about six months, one fine day, she rang me up to break the good news that she was pregnant.

(6)

Shri Jugalkishore Sharma, an industrialist, was a self-made man. His incessant hard work and sharp acumen had led him from a slum to a posh bungalow. He shuddered in his veins and tears rolled from his eyes whenever he was reminded of his unhappy past.

Guided by the considerations of his own unhappy past, Jugalkishore tried to bring up both his children in the best possible way. They were instantly offered whatever they demanded. Chocolates and sweets were always within their reach. Their pockets were always loaded with dry fruits. Every meal was like a feast. Such eating habits led both the children to obesity. They developed elephantine bodies from their very childhood.

They managed to complete their school education without much difficulty. But as they entered the portals of college, other students started making fun of them and their embarrassment knew no bounds. As a result of this, they developed inferiority complexes. When Jugalkishore came to know about the problems of his children, he realized the need to reduce their weight. He made several attempts in this direction but met with no success.

I also tried to treat their obesity, but it was without much success. Both the children had developed carbohydrate addiction and consequently they were unable to implement any dietary-regimen properly.

At last, I advised Jugalkishore to take his children to a competent hypnotist. This advice worked well. The hypnotist took them into a trance and gave them post-hypnotic suggestions that they would develop aversion for carbohydrates. Their inner minds grasped these suggestions well. Thereafter I prescribed a dietery-regimen for them and also advised some exercises. At last, our efforts met with success.

Shri Pravinchandra Shah, aged 50, was a chartered accountant. He had his office in the prestigious Fort area of Mumbai.

Once during a routine pathological investigation of his urine and blood, it was revealed that he had diabetes. Pravinbhai lost his peace of mind. He knew that diabetes was a dreadful disease. Some of his family members had a previous history of this disease.

Besides medical treatment for diabetes, Pravinbhai was also advised to reduce his weight. As Pravinbhai was over-zealous, he almost starved himself. Due to very little food intake and drugs to control diabetes, within three days he developed complaints like headache, giddiness, weakness, etc. One day, he felt so giddy in his office that he lost his balance and fell down. But luckily, he escaped any injury.

But after this event, he was frightened and rushed to me. I too could understand his anxiety to reduce his weight. I explained to him that he should follow the right method for reducing weight. I advised him to increase his food intake and do certain exercises. I also advised him to come to my centre for exercises if it was convenient to him. He readily accepted my advice.

In this way, without much difficulty, we could reduce his weight through dieting and exercises alone, without the help of any drugs.

(8)

One day, a fat young girl aged 18-19 named Kavita Rooparel came to me. Given below is the gist of her complaints which she narrated with great embarrassment: Her weight had been increasing steadily since her very childhood and consequently she was suffering from an inferiority complex. She was not able to socialize properly with her peers. Many a times she was the target of their fun and jokes. She had developed some troubles of menstruation since last 4-5 years. She was overweight by about 20%.

I prepared a diet-and-exercise chart and gave it to her. But in spite of our efforts, there was no significant reduction in her weight. I also confirmed the fact that she was following the programme strictly. Then I suspected that some psychological factor was at work. So I sent her to a psychiatrist friend.

Next day the psychiatrist friend sent me his report: 'When Kavita was 8 years old, she had suddenly come upon a scene in which she found her stepmother making love to her paramour. Their relationship later continued and developed. Kavita could not utter a word about it to anyone. But in her mind, she developed hatred for all men.

As she grew old, layers of fat began to accumulate on her body. It was her subconscious mind that wished to hide her beauty under the cover of obesity so that she would remain away from men.

Thereafter, psychological treatment, coupled with dietary restrictions and exercise brought about the desired weight-loss.

(9)

The case of Shri Mohammadbhai Patel was quite interesting.

When he came to me, he didn't appear to be much overweight. Narrating his trouble he said that to treat his chronic cough and high-blood-pressure, his doctor had advised him to give up smoking. But after he had stopped smoking, he had started putting on weight. He knew well that weight-gain at an advanced age was not a healthy sign.

I tried to console him by saying that there was no need for him to worry as his experience was a common one which many other people in similar predicament had to face.

Taking into consideration the condition of his heart and cardio-vascular system, it was not advisable to prescribe exercises for him. So I suggested some changes in his diet. I advised him to take low carbohydrate, medium-fat and high-protein diet along with plenty of fruits and vegetables. As he was only slightly overweight, it was not necessary to impose any cut on the total quantity of his food-intake.

The experiment of making changes not in the quantity but in the quality of the diet yielded a positive result. Mohammadbhai lost considerable amount of weight. As a result of the weight-loss his blood-pressure also came under control; the efficiency of his heart increased and his complaint of breathlessness also disappeared. Thereafter, I advised him to undertake exercises and increase them gradually.

(10)

Smt. Bhavana Gandhi was married only six months back. At the time of her marriage, she was not overweight. But soon afterwards, she had started putting on weight.

Her husband often advised her to undertake dieting. Bhavana too tried to follow his advice. But she noticed that the weight she lost by dieting was regained during her menstruation days. So she was disappointed by the futility of her attempts and gave up dieting several times.

At last, she came to me and narrated her woes. I explained to her that weight-gain during menstruation period was something normal, due to retention of fluids in the body in those days. For Bhavana, this was something she had never heard of. I asked her to ignore her periodic weight-gain and continue her dieting programme. I also gave her a diet-chart and advised her to do some exercises. Bhavana continued her dieting continuously for three months and restored her body to shapeliness.

APPENDIX 1: CALORIE COUNTER FOR COMMON UNCOOKED FOODS

Sr. No.	Name of the Food	Moisture in %	Protein in %	Fat in %	Carbohydrate in %	Minerals in %	Fibres in %	Calcium in %	Phosphorus in %	Iron in mg per 100 g	Vitamin 'A' in international units per 100g	Vitamin 'B' in international units per 100g	Vitamin 'C' in international units per 100g	Calories per 100g
	Cereals													
1	Wheat	12.8	11.8	1.5	71.2	1.5	1.2	0.05	0.32	5.3	108	180	......	348
2	Rice (machine polished)	13.0	6.9	0.4	79.2	0.5	......	0.01	0.11	1.0	0	20	......	348
3	Rice (hand pounded)	12.2	8.5	0.6	78.0	0.7	......	0.01	0.17	2.8	4	60	......	351
4	Barley	12.5	11.5	1.3	69.3	1.5	3.9	0.03	0.23	3.7	......	150	......	335
5	Kaffircorn (Jowar)	11.9	10.4	1.9	74.0	1.8	......	0.03	0.28	6.2	136	115	......	357
6	Rice (flakes) (Pauva)	12.2	6.6	1.2	78.2	1.8	......	0.02	0.22	8.0	......	70	......	350
7	Bajri (Millet)	12.4	11.6	5.0	67.1	2.7	1.2	0.05	0.35	8.8	220	110	......	360
8	Maize (Corn) (Makai)	14.9	11.1	3.6	66.2	1.5	2.7	0.01	0.33	2.1	......	......	......	342
9	Maize Bhutta (Corn) (Makai Bhutta)	79.4	4.3	0.5	15.1	0.7	......	0.01	0.10	0.7	42	......	......	23
10	Samo (Panicum frumentaceum)	11.9	6.2	2.2	65.5	4.4	9.8	0.02	0.28	2.9	trace	......	......	307
	Pulses													
11	Black gram (Udad)	10.9	24.0	1.4	60.3	3.4	......	0.20	0.37	9.8	64	140	......	348
12	Bengal gram (Chana)	9.8	17.1	5.3	61.2	2.7	3.9	0.19	0.24	9.8	316	100	......	316
13	Bengal gram (roasted)	11.2	22.5	5.2	58.9	2.2	......	0.07	0.31	8.9	......	......	......	372
14	Cow pea (Chouli)	12.7	23.4	1.3	59.7	2.9	......	0.08	0.43	4.3	......	......	......	344

15	Red gram (Tuver : tur)	15.2	22.3	1.7	57.2	3.6	......	0.14	0.26	8.8	220	150	......	334
16	Green gram (Moong)	10.4	24.0	1.3	56.6	3.6	4.1	0.14	0.28	8.4	158	155	......	334
17	Lentil (Masur)	12.4	25.1	0.7	59.7	2.1	......	0.13	0.25	2.0	450	150	......	346
18	Peas	16.0	19.7	1.1	56.6	2.1	4.5	0.07	0.30	4.4	......	150	......	315
19	Field beans (Vaal)	9.6	24.9	0.8	60.1	3.2	1.4	0.06	0.45	2.0	trace	......	......	347
20	Soyabean	20.9	43.2	19.5	20.9	4.6	3.7	0.24	0.69	11.5	710	300	......	432
	Tubers and Edible roots													
21	Colocasia (Alavi)	73.1	3.0	0.1	22.1	1.7	......	0.04	0.14	2.1	40	80	trace	101
22	Ginger	80.9	2.3	0.9	12.3	1.2	2.4	0.02	0.06	2.6	67	......	6	67
23	Onions	86.8	1.2	0.1	11.6	0.4	......	0.18	0.05	0.7	......	40	11	51
24	Carrots	86.0	0.9	0.2	10.7	1.1	1.2	0.08	0.53	1.5	200 to 4300	60	3	47
25	Potatoes	74.7	1.6	0.1	22.9	1.6	......	0.01	0.03	0.7	40	20	17	99
26	Beetroot	83.8	1.7	0.1	13.6	0.8	......	0.20	0.06	1.0	trace	70	88	62
27	Radish	94.4	0.7	0.1	4.2	0.4	......	0.05	0.03	0.04	3	60	15	21
28	Sweet Potatoes (Ratalu)	68.5	1.2	0.3	31.0	1.0	......	0.02	0.05	0.8	10	......	24	132
29	Garlic	62.8	6.3	0.1	29.0	1.0	0.8	0.03	0.31	1.3	0	......	13	142
30	Yam (Suran)	78.7	1.2	0.1	18.4	0.8	......	0.05	0.02	0.6	434	20	trace	79
	Nuts and Oilseeds													
31	Walnut (Akhrot)	4.5	15.6	64.5	11.0	1.8	2.6	0.10	0.38	4.8	10	150	0	687
32	Linseed (Alasi)	6.6	20.3	37.1	28.8	2.4	4.8	0.17	0.37	2.7	50	......	0	530
33	Cashew nut (Kaju)	5.9	21.2	46.9	22.3	2.4	1.3	0.05	0.45	5.0	100	......	0	596
34	Coconut	36.3	4.5	41.6	13.0	1.0	3.6	0.01	0.24	1.7	trace	15	1	444
35	Til	5.1	18.3	43.3	25.2	5.2	2.9	1.45	0.57	10.5	100	......	0	564
36	Pistachio nut (Pista)	5.6	19.8	53.5	16.2	2.8	2.1	0.14	0.43	13.7	240	......	0	626

Sr. No.	Name of the Food	Moisture in %	Protein in %	Fat in %	Carbohydrate in %	Minerals in %	Fibres in %	Calcium in %	Phosphorus in %	Iron in mg per 100 g	Vitamin 'A' in inter-national units per 100g	Vitamin 'B' in inter-national units per 100g	Vitamin 'C' in inter-national units per 100g	Calories per 100 g
37	Almond nut (Badam)	5.2	20.8	58.9	10.5	2.0	1.7	0.23	0.49	3.5	trace	80	0	655
38	Ground nut (Peanut) (Moongfali)	7.9	26.7	40.1	20.3	1.9	3.1	0.05	0.39	1.6	63	300	0	549
39	Mustard seeds (Rai)	8.5	22.0	39.7	23.8	4.2	1.8	0.49	0.70	17.9	270	......	trace	541
	Fruits													
40	Pineapple (Ananas)	86.5	7.6	0.1	12.0	0.5	0.3	0.02	0.01	0.9	60	......	63	50
41	Indian gooseberry (Amala)	81.2	0.5	0.1	14.1	0.7	3.4	0.05	0.02	1.2	......	......	600	59
42	Fig (Anjeer)	80.8	1.3	0.2	17.1	0.6	......	0.06	0.03	1.2	270	......	2	75
43	Tamarind (ripe) (Amli)	20.9	3.1	0.1	67.4	2.9	5.6	0.17	0.11	10.9	100	......	13	283
44	Watermelon (Kalinger)	95.7	0.1	0.2	3.8	0.2	......	0.11	0.01	0.2	trace	......	1	17
45	Raisins (dry) (Kismis)	18.5	2.0	0.2	77.3	2.0	......	0.10	0.08	4.0	0	75	trace	319
46	Mangoes (raw)	90.0	0.7	0.1	7.6	0.4	......	0.01	0.03	1.7	trace	......	1	39
47	Mangoes (ripe)	86.1	0.6	0.1	8.8	0.3	1.1	0.01	0.02	4.5	4800	......	......	50
48	Bananas	61.4	1.3	0.2	36.4	0.7	......	0.01	0.05	0.4	trace	50	1	153
49	Wood apple	69.5	7.3	0.6	15.5	1.9	5.2	0.13	0.11	0.6	......	......	......	97
50	Dates (Khajoor)	26.1	3.0	0.2	67.3	1.3	2.1	0.07	0.08	10.6	600	30	trace	283
51	Pompelmoose	92.0	0.7	0.1	7.1	0.2	......	0.02	0.02	0.2	......	40	31	32
52	Guava (Amrood)	76.1	1.5	0.2	14.5	0.8	6.9	0.01	0.04	1.0	trace	......	299	66

53	Rose apple (Jambu)	78.2	0.7	0.1	19.7	0.4	0.9	0.02	0.01	1.0	......	......	......	83
54	Tomatoes (ripe)	94.5	1.0	0.1	3.9	0.5	......	0.01	0.02	0.1	320	40	32	20
55	Pomegranates (Anar)	78.0	1.6	0.1	14.6	0.7	5.1	0.01	0.07	0.3	0	......	16	65
56	Grapes	85.5	0.8	0.1	10.2	0.4	3.0	3.03	0.02	0.4	15	trace	3	45
57	Pears	86.9	0.2	0.1	11.5	0.3	1.0	0.01	0.01	0.7	14	......	trace	47
58	Papaya	89.6	0.5	0.1	9.5	0.4	......	0.01	0.01	0.4	2020	......	46	40
59	Peach	90.1	1.5	0.2	8.9	0.6	......	0.02	0.02	1.5	230	40	1	38
60	Jack-fruit (Fanas)	77.2	1.9	0.2	17.4	0.8	1.1	0.17	0.11	10.9	100	......	03	65
61	Jujube fruit (Bor)	85.9	0.8	0.1	12.8	0.4	......	0.03	0.03	0.8	70	......	......	55
62	Mosambi	84.6	1.5	1.0	10.9	0.7	1.3	0.09	0.02	0.3	26	......	63	59
63	Raspberry	82.7	1.8	0.2	11.5	0.6	3.2	0.01	0.06	1.8	......	......	49	55
64	Lemon	85.0	1.0	0.9	11.1	0.3	1.7	0.07	0.01	2.3	trace	......	39	57
65	Apple	85.9	0.3	0.1	13.4	0.3	......	0.01	0.02	1.7	trace	40	2	56
66	Orange	87.8	0.9	0.3	10.6	0.4	......	0.05	0.02	0.01	350	40	68	49
	Vegetables													
67	Cucumber	96.4	0.4	0.1	2.8	0.3	......	0.01	0.03	1.5	trace	90	7	14
68	Bitter gourd (Karela)	92.4	1.6	0.2	4.2	0.8	0.8	0.02	0.07	2.2	210	24	88	25
69	Plantains (raw-bananas)	83.2	1.4	0.2	14.7	0.5	......	0.01	0.03	0.6	50	15	24	66
70	Plantain flowers	90.2	1.5	0.2	5.0	1.2	1.9	0.03	0.05	0.1	......	......	......	28
71	Cabbage	90.2	1.8	0.1	6.3	0.6	1.0	0.03	0.05	0.8	2000	150	124	30
72	Cauliflower	89.4	3.5	0.4	5.3	1.4	......	0.03	0.06	1.3	38	110	37	39
73	Pumpkin (gourd)	92.6	1.4	0.1	5.3	0.6	......	0.01	0.03	0.7	84	200	2	28
74	Cluster beans	82.5	3.7	0.2	9.9	1.4	2.3	0.13	0.05	5.8	330	......	48	56
75	Chola pods	92.5	0.9	0.1	3.5	1.8	1.2	0.26	0.03	1.8	......	......	......	18
76	Tomatoes (raw)	92.8	1.9	0.1	4.5	0.7	......	0.02	0.04	2.4	320	23	31	27

Sr. No.	Name of the Food	Moisture in %	Protein in %	Fat in %	Carbohydrate in %	Minerals in %	Fibres in %	Calcium in %	Phosphorus in %	Iron in mg per 100 g	Vitamin 'A' in inter-national units per 100g	Vitamin 'B' in inter-national units per 100g	Vitamin 'C' in inter-national units per 100g	Calories per 100g
77	Tomatoes (ripe)	94.5	1.0	0.1	3.9	0.5	.....	0.01	0.02	0.1	320	40	33	20
78	Tindora	92.3	1.7	0.1	5.2	0.6	.....	0.02	0.03	0.9	28	.....	.....	27
79	Ridge gourd	95.4	0.5	0.1	3.7	0.3	.....	0.04	0.04	1.6	56	22	.....	18
80	Bottle gourd	96.3	0.2	0.1	2.9	0.5	.....	0.02	0.01	0.7	trace	.....	.....	13
81	Parval (long)	94.1	0.5	0.3	4.4	0.7	.....	0.05	0.03	1.3	160	.....	trace	22
82	Parval (ordinary)	92.3	2.0	0.3	1.9	0.5	3.0	0.03	0.04	1.7	.....	.....	.....	18
83	Broad beans (Papadi)	82.4	4.5	0.1	10.0	1.0	2.0	0.05	0.06	1.6	.....	.....	12	59
84	French beans	82.0	1.7	0.1	4.5	1.0	1.8	0.05	0.03	1.7	221	144	14	30
85	Lady's finger	88.0	2.2	0.2	7.7	0.7	1.2	0.09	0.08	1.5	58	21	16	41
86	Brinjals	91.5	1.3	0.3	6.4	0.5	.....	0.02	0.06	1.3	5	15	23	34
87	Peas	72.1	7.2	0.1	19.8	0.8	.....	0.02	0.08	1.5	139	120	9	109
88	Turnip (Salgam)	91.1	0.5	0.2	7.6	0.6	.....	0.03	0.04	0.4	trace	40	43	34
89	Drumsticks	86.9	2.5	0.1	4.3	2.0	4.8	0.01	0.03	0.6	trace	.....	18	20
	Leafy Vegetables													
90	Bishop's weed (Ajawan leaves)	81.3	6.0	0.6	8.6	2.1	1.4	0.23	0.14	6.3	5800 to 7500	trace	62	64
91	Alavi leaves	89.4	0.3	0.3	4.2	1.2	0.6	0.06	0.02	0.5	.....	.....	.....	20
92	Carrot leaves	83.3	5.1	0.5	8.3	2.8	.....	0.34	0.11	8.8	.....	.....	.....	58
93	Gram leaves	77.8	7.0	1.4	11.7	2.1	.....	0.34	0.12	23.8	.....	.....	.....	90
94	Tanka leaves	87.9	4.7	0.4	3.7	3.3	.....	0.15	0.08	4.2	.....	.....	.....	37
95	Onion leaves	87.6	0.9	0.2	8.9	0.8	1.6	0.05	0.05	7.5	.....	.....	.....	41

96	Hermaphrodite leaves (Tandaljo leaves)	85.0	3.0	0.3	8.1	3.6	......	0.08	0.05	22.9	......	......	......	47
97	Hermaphrodite (amnth) (Tandaljo leaves) (red)	85.8	4.9	0.5	5.7	3.1	......	0.50	0.10	21.4	2500 to 11000	173	173	47
98	Coriander leaves	87.9	3.3	0.6	6.5	1.7	......	0.14	0.06	10.0	10460 to 12600	......	135	45
99	Betel leaves	85.4	3.1	0.8	6.1	2.3	2.3	0.23	0.04	5.7	9600	......	5	44
100	Spinach leaves (Palakh leaves)	91.7	1.9	0.9	4.0	1.5	......	0.06	0.01	5.0	2600 to 3500	70	48	32
101	Mint leaves	83.0	4.8	0.6	8.0	1.6	2.0	0.20	0.08	15.6	2700	......	......	57
102	Fenugreek leaves (Methi leaves)	81.8	4.9	0.9	9.8	1.6	1.0	0.47	0.05	16.9	3900	70	......	67
103	Mustard seeds leaves	84.9	5.1	0.4	7.1	2.5	......	0.37	0.11	12.5	......	......	......	55
104	Nimb leaves (tender)	59.4	11.6	3.0	21.2	2.6	2.2	0.13	0.19	25.3	4600	......	......	158
105	Lettuce	92.9	2.1	0.3	3.0	1.2	0.5	0.05	0.03	2.4	2200	90	15	23
106	Drumstick tree leaves	75.0	6.7	1.7	13.4	2.3	0.9	0.44	0.07	7.0	11300	70	220	94
	Spices and Condiments													
107	Ajawan	8.9	15.4	18.1	38.6	7.1	11.9	1.42	0.30	14.6	......	......	......	379
108	Cardamom (Elaichi)	20.0	10.2	2.2	42.1	5.4	20.1	0.13	0.16	5.0	......	......	0	229
109	Nutmeg (Jaiphal)	14.3	7.5	36.4	28.5	1.7	11.6	0.12	0.24	4.6	trace	......	0	472
110	Mace (Jawantri)	15.9	6.5	24.4	47.8	1.6	3.8	0.18	0.10	12.6	......	......	0	437
111	Cumin seeds (Jeera)	11.9	18.7	15.0	36.6	5.8	12.0	1.08	0.49	31.0	870	......	3	356
112	Coriander seeds	11.2	14.1	16.1	21.6	4.4	32.6	0.63	0.37	17.9	1570	......	trace	288
113	Chillies	10.0	15.9	6.2	31.6	6.1	30.2	0.16	0.37	2.3	576	......	50	246

Sr. No.	Name of the Food	Moisture in %	Protein in %	Fat in %	Carbohydrate in %	Minerals in %	Fibres in %	Calcium in %	Phosphorus in %	Iron in mg per 100 g	Vitamin 'A' in international units per 100g	Vitamin 'B' in international units per 100g	Vitamin 'C' in international units per 100g	Calories per 100 g
114	Chillies (green)	82.6	2.9	0.6	6.1	1.0	6.8	0.03	0.08	1.2	454	......	111	41
115	Pepper (black)	12.9	11.5	6.8	49.5	4.4	14.9	0.46	0.20	16.8	......	......	......	305
116	Fenugreek seeds (Methi)	13.7	26.2	5.8	44.1	3.0	7.2	0.16	0.37	14.1	160	......	0	333
117	Mustard Seeds (Rai)	8.5	22.0	39.7	23.8	4.2	1.8	0.49	0.70	17.9	270	......	trace	541
118	Cloves	23.3	5.2	8.9	47.9	5.2	9.5	0.74	0.10	4.9	......	......	0	293
119	Turmeric	13.1	6.3	5.1	69.4	3.5	2.6	0.15	0.28	18.6	50	......	0	349
120	Asafoetida	16.0	4.0	1.1	67.8	7.0	4.1	0.69	0.05	22.2	......	......	0	297
	Milk and Milk preparations													
121	Milk (Cow's)	87.6	3.3	3.6	4.8	0.7	......	0.12	0.09	0.2	180	17	2	65
122	Milk (Buffalo's)	81.0	4.3	8.8	5.1	0.8	......	0.21	0.13	0.2	162	......	......	117
123	Milk (goat's)	85.2	3.7	5.6	4.7	0.8	......	0.17	0.12	0.3	182	......	2	84
124	Milk (human)	88.0	1.0	3.9	7.0	0.1	......	0.02	0.01	0.2	208	......	2	67
125	Milk (human) (b.s.)*	92.1	2.5	1.0	4.6	0.7	......	0.12	0.09	0.2	......	......	1	29
126	Milk powder (b.s.)*	......	38.0	0.1	51.0	......	......	......	......	......	......	......	......	357
127	Curd (made from cow's milk)	90.3	2.9	2.9	3.3	0.6	......	0.12	0.09	0.3	130	......	......	51
128	Buttermilk	97.5	0.8	1.1	0.5	0.1	......	0.03	0.03	0.8	trace	......	......	15
*	Butter separated.													

Sr. No.	Name of the Food	Moisture in %	Protein in %	Fat in %	Carbohydrate in %	Minerals in %	Fibres in %	Calcium in %	Phosphorus in %	Iron in mg per 100 g	Vitamin 'A' in international units per 100g	Vitamin 'B' in international units per 100g	Vitamin 'C' in international units per 100g	Calories per 100g
129	Paneer	40.3	24.1	25.1	6.3	4.2	......	0.79	0.52	0.1	273	......	......	348
130	Khoya (made from buffalo's milk)	30.6	14.6	31.2	20.5	3.1	......	0.65	0.42	5.8	......	......	0	421
131	Khoya (made from buffalo's milk) (b.s.)*	46.1	22.3	1.6	25.7	4.3	......	0.99	0.65	2.7	......	......	0	206
	Non-Veg. food													
132	Egg (duck's)	71.0	13.5	13.7	0.7	1.0	......	0.07	0.26	3.0	1200	......	......	180
133	Egg (hen's)	73.7	13.3	13.3	......	1.0	......	0.06	0.22	2.1	1200	......	......	173
134	Liver (sheep's)	70.4	19.3	7.5	1.4	1.5	......	0.01	0.38	6.3	22300	120	20	150
135	Honey	......	0.4	......	71.3	......	......	......	......	......	trace	trace	trace	437
136	Fish (small)	77.5	21.5	1.6	......	2.0	......	0.06	0.41	2.3	26	60	......	100
137	Fish (big)	78.4	22.6	0.6	......	0.8	......	0.02	0.19	0.9	......	......	......	91
138	Shrimp (zinga)	77.9	20.8	0.3	......	1.4	......	0.09	0.24	0.8	trace	30	......	86
139	Meat (prawns)	83.5	8.9	1.1	3.4	3.2	......	1.37	0.15	21.2	1300	......	......	59
140	Beef	74.3	22.6	2.6	......	1.0	......	0.01	0.19	0.8	trace	50	2	114
141	Mutton	71.5	18.5	13.3	......	1.3	......	0.15	0.15	2.5	31	60	......	194
142	Pork	77.4	18.7	4.4	......	1.0	......	0.03	0.20	2.3	trace	180	2	114
*	Butter separated.													

APPENDIX 2 : CALORIE COUNTER FOR COOKED OR PROCESSED COMMON FOODS

Sr. No.	Food Item	Approx. Quantity	Calorie
1	Chapati (Millet) (Small)	45 g	108
2	Chapati (Jowar) (small)	45 g	106
3	Chapati (Wheat) (thin)	20 g	40
4	Poori (Wheat)	16 g	68
5	Khakhara (Wheat)	20 g	40
6	Paratha (Wheat)	55 g	304
7	Bread (two slices)	45 g	120
8	Wheat biscuits (two)	20 g	64
9	Khichri/Rice	140 g	238
10	Dal (Watery) (one small bowl)	200 g	105
11	Jam (one spoon)	20 g	58
12	Jelly (one spoon)	20 g	52
13	Squash (Orange/Lemon)	one glass	69
14	Squash (Mango)	one glass	72
15	Butter (one spoon)	5 g	36
16	Cream (one spoon)	15 g	50
17	Ghee (one spoon)	5 g	45
18	Groundnut oil (one spoon)	15 g	126
19	Paneer (one spoon)	30 g	112
20	Ice cream	100 g	196
21	Horlicks, Bournvita, etc. (two spoons)		110
22	Cake (without icing) (one piece)	75 g	218
23	Cake (with icing) (one piece)	90 g	302
24	Pie	160 g	377
25	Pudding (1/2 cup)	105 g	185
26	Idli (1 piece)	68 g	65
27	Upama (one plate)	260 g	397
28	Sada Dosa (one)	100 g	216
29	Masala Dosa	100 g	210
30	Potato Bhajia (four)	60 g	240
31	Onion Bhajia (six)	60 g	197
32	Potato Chips (ten)	20 g	108
33	Pattis (one)	60 g	201
34	Potato Wada (one)	45 g	118
35	Dahi Wada (one)	45 g	83
36	Kachori (one)	45 g	190
37	Cutlets (one)	60 g	126
38	Potato Pauva (1 plate)	60 g	123
39	Sago Khichri (one plate)	45 g	182
40	Samosa (one)	30 g	103
41	Chakari (one)	30 g	170
42	Mesur (one piece)	56 g	345
43	Boondi Laddu (one)	35 g	150
44	Carrot Halwa	85 g	333
45	Dudhi Halwa	85 g	300
46	Glucose (one spoon)	75 g	218
47	Honey (one spoon)	21 g	66
48	Jaggery (one spoon)	15 g	56
49	Sugar (one spoon)	6 g	25
	Non-veg. food items		
50	Egg gravy (one cup)	150 g	181
51	Omlet (one)	40 g	77
52	Fried fish	100 g	245
53	Fried meat	140 g	340
54	Soup (Chicken, Mutton)	200 g	35
	Beverages		
55	Tea (one cup)	150 g	60
56	Coffee (one cup)	150 g	75
57	Lime juice (one glass)	200 g	75
58	Aerated Drinks (Thums up, Gold Spot, etc.) (one bottle)	200 g	80
59	Beer (one glass)	200 g	100
60	Alcohol (one peg)	45 g	110

APPENDIX 3 : VITAMINS

Vitamin	Daily requirement of an adult person	Function	Sources	Symptoms of Deficiency
Vitamin 'A'	4000 to 5000 international units	This Vitamin is essential for the preservation and growth of certain cells in the body. It is also essential for preserving health of the eyesight. Our night-vision depends on this vitamin. Besides, it is also essential for the general development of bones and formation of teeth.	Milk, paneer, leafy vegetables, cabbage, carrots, red and yellow vegetables and fruits. Besides, it is also available in large quantities from the liver oil of certain fishes. (e.g., cod-liver oil)	Lack of Vitamin 'A' causes slackening of the growth of body. Eyes and skin become dry; night-vision is impaired; abnormalities of bone and teeth also develop.
Vitamin 'B' **Note:** This is a group of Vitamins comprising eight Vitamins (Vitamins B_1, B_2, B_6, B_{12} Niacin, Pantothenic acid, Biotin, and Folecin)	Each approximately 0.5 to 5 mg	Vitamins of this group are essential for the growth of the body, for causing appetite, and for the health of eyesight, nervous system and skin. They are also essential for preventing anaemia.	Milk, yeast, wheat bran, sprouted wheat, greenleaf vegetables, cereals, etc. eggs, meat (particularly liver) and fish are also sources of Vitamin 'B'.	Lack of Vitamin 'B' causes a disease named Beriberi. Lack of Vitamin 'B' causes cracks in the skin and around eyes, nose and mouth. Lack of Niacin causes a disease called Pellagra and abnormalities of the nervous system. Lack of B_6 causes anaemia and skin diseases. Lack of Pantothenic acid causes metabolic disorders. Symptoms of Biotin and Folecin are similar to those of the lack of Pantothenic acid. Lack of Vitamin B_{12} causes slackening of the growth of the body and also causes fatal anaemia.

Vitamin	Daily requirement of an adult person	Function	Sources	Symptoms of Deficiency
Vitamin 'C'	45 mg	This vitamin is essential for the growth of body. It also makes a vital contribution to the formation of teeth and bones. It helps in keeping the different cells connected to one another. It expedites the process of healing wounds. It enhances the resistance power of the body. It is also associated with the production of Steroid hormones in the body.	Sweet and sour (citrous) fruits, Indian gooseberry (amla), tomatoes, watermelon, guava, cabbage, pineapples, potatoes and green-leafy vegetables are some of the sources of Vitamin 'C'.	Besides causing a disease called scurvy; lack of this vitamin may cause problems of teeth and gums, internal haemorrhage, osteoporosis of bones, weight loss and infertility.
Vitamin 'D'	300 to 400 international units.	This vitamin is essential for the growth of body. It also makes a vital contribution to the formation of teeth and bones.	Sunlight is the best source of Vitamin 'D'. Besides that, it is also available from milk, eggs, and some fish-liver oils.	Deficiency of Vitamin 'D' causes osteoporosis of bones and consequently children develop a disease called Rickets.
Vitamin 'E'	12 to 15 international units.	This is an essential vitamin for fertility. Besides that, it also strengthens red blood cells and prevents their disintegration.	Milk, sprouted wheat, green leafy vegetables, vegetable oils, dry fruits (nuts) and eggs.	Deficiency of this vitamin may cause infertility.
Vitamin 'K'	1 to 2 mg	It is essential for producing Prothombin–a substance that is necessary for coagulation of blood.	Wheat bran, green leafy vegetables, tomatoes, cauliflower, soyabean oil, vegetable oils and animal livers.	Lack of this vitamin hampers the production of Prothombin and consequently blood coagulation does not take place, as a result of which, there is profuse bleeding even after a minor injury.

APPENDIX 4 : MINERALS

Mineral	Daily requirement of an adult person	Functions	Sources	Symptoms of Deficiency
Calcium	800 mg	About 99 % calcium is in the teeth and bones. It is also essential for free movement of different substances in the cells of body.	Milk and milk preparations, fenugreek, drumstick and similar other leafy vegetables, beetroot, figs, grapes, watermelon, bajri (millet), til, black gram (udad). Besides these, calcium is available from some types of fish and oyster also.	Lack of calcium causes weakening of bones & teeth and also causes osteoporosis.
Phosphorus	800 mg	About 80 % phosphorus is contained in the bones and teeth. It is a vital component of every cells in the body. It helps in maintaining blood pH. Besides, it is also essential for producing vital substances like DNA, RNA and ATP.	Milk, paneer, yeast, dry fruits (nuts), soyabean, dates, carrots, guava, etc. Besides these, it is also available from eggs, fish and meat. .	Calcium deficiency causes weakening of bones and weight loss.
Potassium	2500 mg	Potassium is an important component of the intracellular fluid. It is essential for the metabolism of carbohydrates and proteins. It also helps in maintaining blood pH.	Fresh fruits, milk, garlic, radish, potatoes and meat contain potassium in large quantities.	Potassium deficiency may cause weakening of muscles, brittleness of bones, infertility and cardiac trouble.

Mineral	Daily requirement of an adult person	Functions	Sources	Symptoms of Deficiency
Sodium	2500 mg	Sodium is an important component of the extracellular fluid. About 30 to 40 % sodium is contained in the bones.	Salt, milk, beetroot, carrots, radish, French beans, etc. contain sodium. Besides them, it is also found in eggs, meat and fish.	Sodium deficiency causes headache, nausea, slow growth of body and muscular weakness.
Iron	10 mg	About 70 % iron is contained in the haemoglobin. The remaining 26 % is contained in the liver, spleen and bones. In absence of iron, cells of the body cannot exchange oxygen.	Fenugreek, mint and similar other green-leafy vegetables, til, bajri (millet), gram, green gram, black gram, soyabean, dates, mangoes, etc. Besides these, it is also obtained from eggs, meat, animal livers, oysters, etc.	Anaemia is the main symptom of iron deficiency.
Sulphur	300 mg	Sulphur is a component of proteins and some vitamins. It is essential for metabolic process in the body.	Beetroot, cabbage, garlic, onions, milk and non-veg. food are some of the chief sources of sulphur.	Sulphur deficiency causes metabolic disorders in the body.
Magnesium	350 mg	About 50 % magnesium is contained in the bones. The remaining 50 % is contained in the cells. It activates many enzymes in the body and that is why many processes of the body depend on it.	Milk, grains, green vegetables, dry fruits (nuts) and meat contains magnesium.	Magnesium deficiency causes weakening of bones, teeth and muscles. Lack of magnesium may also create cardiac problems.

Mineral	Daily requirement of an adult person	Functions	Sources	Symptoms of Deficiency
Chlorine	2000 mg	This substance works in collaboration with sodium. It is an important component of extracellular fluid. It also activates many enzymes in the body. It is an important component of gastric juices responsible for the digestion of food.	Salt, milk, carrots, apricot, beetroots, French beans, potatoes, spinach, cabbage, tomatoes, bananas, dates, etc. contain chlorine. Besides them, it is also obtained from eggs, meat and sea-fish.	Chlorine deficiency weakens the bones and makes the joints stiff.
Iodine	0.14 mg	It is a component of thyroid gland secretion.	It can be obtained from sea-food and green-leafy vegetables.	Iodine deficiency causes thyroid gland disorders and a disease named Goitre.

APPENDIX 5 : SUBSTITUTE FOODS

FRUITS

Following are the substitutes of an orange:

One small apple
One fig
One small guava
One small mosambi
One small chikoo
One medium size peach
Half a mango (ripe)
One-third banana
14 to 15 grapes
One slice of pineapple

GRAINS

Following are the substitutes of 30 g (one oz.) of rice:

30 g of wheat flour
30 g of kaffir corn (jowar)
30 g of bajri (millet)
30 g of ragi/vari/sago
30 g of rice flakes (pauva)
30 g of puffed rice (mamra)

CEREALS

Following are the substitutes of 30 g red gram dal (Tuver dal):

30 g of black gram dal
30 g of green gram/green gram dal
30 g of field bean/field bean dal
30 g of Bengal gram/Bengal gram dal
30 g of lentil/lentil dal
30 g of dry peas

FAT

Following are the substitutes of one spoonful of vegetable oil:

One spoon of butter
One spoon of cream
One spoon of ghee (pure)
One spoon of ghee (vegetable)

BREAD-BISCUITS, ETC.

Following are the substitutes of a small bread (30 g):

Two small khakharas
Two small puffed chapatis
Two or three small biscuits (containing little sugar)
One and a half spoonful of rice
One and a half cup of parched corn (Dhani)
One cup of popcorn
One small boiled potato

APPENDIX 6 : MODELS OF DIET

A DIET-PLAN PROVIDING 600 CALORIES PER DAY :

(1) Early morning : One glass of warm water with a few drops of lemon added to it.

(2) Morning breakfast : Any one or two of the following items :

(a) One cup of tea or coffee with a little milk added to it. (Use saccharin instead of sugar.)

(b) any small fruit (except ripe mango or banana)

(c) two or three small tomatoes or cucumbers

(d) Non-vegetarians can take an egg.

(3) Mid-day meal :

(a) First of all, chew properly two or three small cucumbers or tomatoes.

(b) one small chapati

(c) half a bowl of any low-calorie vegetable

(d) half a bowl of moong soup

(e) Non-vegetarians can take a little piece of meat (without fat) or fish.

(4) Afternoon tea/early evening : As per the morning breakfast

(5) Supper : As per the mid-day meal, except for the fact that a small bowlful of rice or khichri can be taken instead of rice.

A DIET-PLAN PROVIDING 800 CALORIES PER DAY :

(1) Early morning : One glass warm water with a few drops of lemon added to it.

(2) Morning breakfast : Any one or two of the following items may be taken :

(a) $\frac{3}{4}$ cup of milk (without sugar) or one cup of tea or coffee with a little milk (Use saccharin as a substitute for sugar.)

(b) half a khakhara

(c) one egg

(d) 2 or 3 small tomatoes or cucumbers

(3) Mid-day meal :

(a) First of all, chew properly 2 or 3 medium-size cucumbers or 4 or 5 tomatoes.

(b) one small chapati or a slice of bread

(c) one small bowl of a vegetable with low calories

(d) one small bowl of moong soup

(e) Non-vegetarians can take some meat (without fat) or a fish.

(4) Afternoon/Early evening: As per the morning breakfast.

(5) Supper: As per the mid-day meal except that half a bowl or rice or khichri may be taken as a substitute for chapatis or bread.

A DIET-PLAN PROVIDING 1200 CALORIES PER DAY:

(1) Early morning: One glass of warm water with a few drops of a lemon added to it.

(2) Morning breakfast: Take any one or two of the following items:

(a) One cup of milk without sugar or one cup of tea or coffee with a little milk. (Use saccharin instead of sugar.)

(b) one small fruit

(c) one khakhara or a slice of bread

(d) one egg

(e) two or three small tomatoes or cucumbers

(3) Mid-day meal:

(a) First of all, before commencing the meal, take one cup of warm clear vegetable soup or any green-leaf soup. Non-vegetarians can take a soup of their liking; but flour should not be used for preparing any soup.

(b) Chew properly 4 or 5 tomatoes or 2 or 3 medium-size cucumbers. This items can be consumed in a larger quantity if desired.

(c) one small bowl of vegetable

(d) two small chapatis or a slice of bread

(e) one small bowl of moong or any other similar cereal

(f) Non-vegetarians can take some meat (without fat) or a fish.

(4) Afternoon/Early evening: As per the morning breakfast.

(5) Supper: As per the mid-day meal except for the fact that one small bowl of khichri or rice can be taken as a substitute for chapatis or bread.

Published by Navneet Publications (India) Ltd., Dantali, Gujarat.
Printed by Navneet Publications (India) Ltd., Dantali, Gujarat.